This is
CATAMARAN
Sailing

This is
CATAMARAN
Sailing

Ernst W. Barth & Klaus J. Enzmann

Foreword by Francis Prout
Translated by John Powell

NAUTICAL

First published in Great Britain 1986 by
NAUTICAL BOOKS
an imprint of A & C Black (Publishers) Ltd
35 Bedford Row, London, WC1R 4JH

Reprinted 1987

ISBN 0 7136 5880 0

Typeset in Great Britain by MJL Typesetting
Services Limited, Hertfordshire.
Printed in Germany

Contents

Foreword

by Francis Prout

I consider it a privilege and it is indeed a pleasure to write the foreword to this book. Having admired the 'This is...' series for a number of years, I am pleased to see that it has turned its attention to catamaran sailing. For thirty-two years now, I have been lucky to experience the exhilaration of sailing on two hulls.

In 1954 my brother, Francis, and I launched our first Shearwater class catamaran and the Shearwater III is still being raced and sailed today with strong fleets in many places throughout the world. There is now a catamaran class in the Olympic games and there are scores of different catamaran classes in use for racing, for fast sailing and for pure fun.

Two keen multihull sailors from Germany have put into book form accumulated knowledge on choosing, setting up and sailing to the best effect these exciting sailing boats. Those new to sailing should certainly give this type of boat a trial amongst all the other present day yachting attractions.

I recommend the pages which follow and wish all catamaran enthusiasts good sailing and steady expansion of the sport.

But why a catamaran?

The question 'Why a multihull?' can be answered quickly and simply with the words 'more speed', but the question 'Why specifically a catamaran?' needs a rather fuller explanation.

Of course, proas and trimarans – the latter a term coined by the Russian Victor Tchetchet, who raced a home-built catamaran against yachts of conventional construction off Kiev in 1909 and won by a wide margin – are also very fast multihull boats. However, it is the catamaran that has come to dominate the sports boat market. Racing trimarans, such as the British Kraken and the Danish Supernovas, have made as little impact on the racing scene as the few proas that have ventured in this direction.

The sketches on page 8 show the various types of open multihulls.

There are other considerations such as comfort, space on board and heavy weather behaviour that are of interest to blue-water skippers but which do not come into play in the racing boat. Nevertheless, the arguments set out below also apply to cruising multihulls.

First of all, we need to understand at least a little physics.

One of the most important factors for the performance of a sailing boat (in other words, for its speed) is it's power-to-weight ratio. This is simple to calculate: add the weight of the boat and the weight of the crew in kilograms and divide the total by the sail area in square metres.

For the Tornado racing catamaran with a 160 kg crew the formula would be as follows:

$$P = \frac{168 + 160}{21.8} = 15.05 \text{ kg/m}^2$$

This Tornado therefore has a power-to-weight ratio of 15.05 kg per square metre.

The fact that weight has a decisive influence on speed is obvious – we know that from the motor car – and even little Jimmy can figure out that boats with a large sail area are faster than ones with less.

Except that it is not quite as simple as that. What is important is not the area of sail set on the mast but the canvas that the boat can carry. This depends on the boat's 'righting moment'. In simple terms, this is the force that the boat and crew can exert to prevent the boat being laid on its beam ends by the pressure of the wind.

The righting moment (M_a) can be calculated by multiplying the weight of the boat (W_1) by the distance between the boat's centre of gravity and its healing axis (D_1) and adding to this the result of the same calculation for the weight of the crew (W_2, W_3) and their distance from the boat's axis (D_2, D_3).

The sketch on page 9 compares the Tornado with the Flying Dutchman racing monohull. The catamaran is the clear winner, with 360 m.kg (metres × kilograms), (5543 ft. lb) more righting moment. This is borne out in practice: once the Tornado can exploit its greater righting power (from about force 2 upwards), it is noticeably faster than the dinghy.

This example also illustrates the doubtful validity of yardstick numbers or similar time correction systems in races between monohulls and multihulls. Since the ratings are only averages of recorded race results, under such a handicapping system a multihull can never win in light airs nor a monohull in strong winds. But let us now turn to the various types of multihull boats.

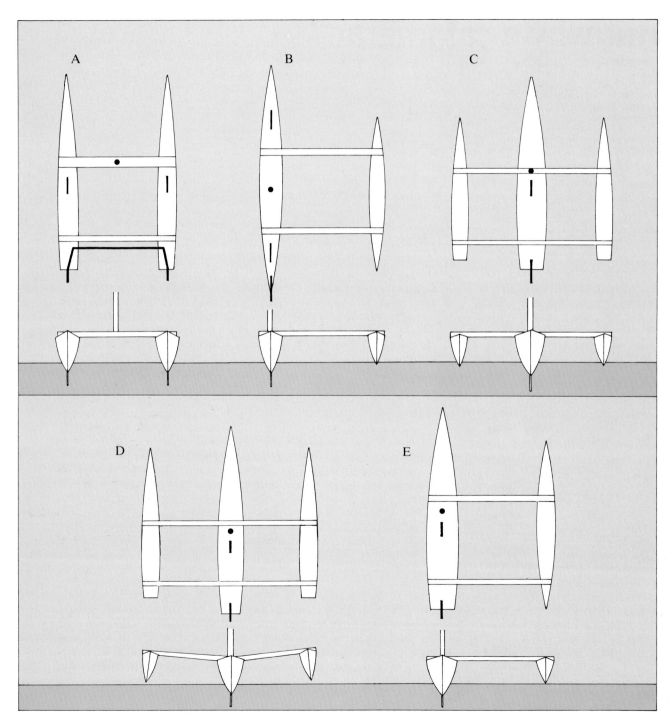

Left.
A. Catamaran, with or without centreboards, with symmetrical or asymmetrical hulls.
B. Traditional proa, with or without centreboards, with symmetrical or asymmetrical hulls; the length of the outrigger is about 50% to 60% of the length of the main hull.
C. Old-style trimaran, with or without a centreboard; the length of the outriggers is about 50% to 60% of the main hull.
D. Newer-style trimaran, with or without a centreboard; the length of the outriggers is about 80% to 90% of the length of the main hull and the crossbeams are angled by up to 20°.
E. Modern proa, with or without a centreboard, with symmetrical or asymmetrical hulls; the outriggers measure about 80% to 90% of the length of the main hull.

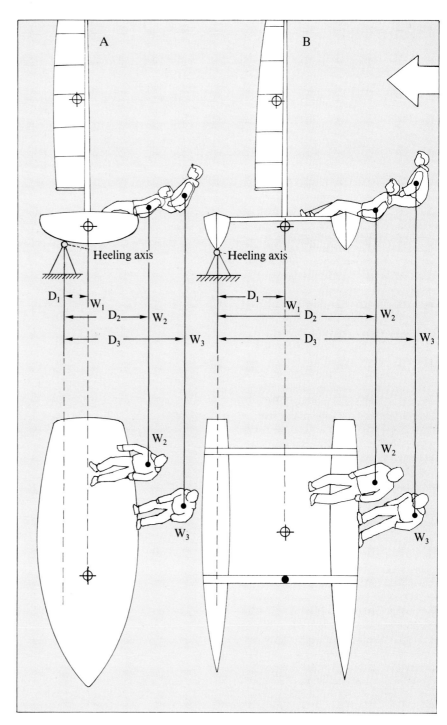

Right.
A. The equation of moments for the FD gives:

$$FD: \sum M_a = \sum \begin{array}{l} W_1 \times D_1 \\ W_2 \times D_2 \ (m \times kg) \\ W_3 \times D_3 \end{array}$$

$$\begin{aligned} &= 160 \times 0.5 \\ &= 80 \times 1.6 \\ &= 80 \times 2.5 \\ &= 408 \ (m.kg) \end{aligned}$$

B. The equation of moments for the Tornado gives:

$$Tornado: \sum M_a = \sum \begin{array}{l} W_1 \times D_1 \\ W_2 \times D_2 \ (m \times kg) \\ W_3 \times D_3 \end{array}$$

$$\begin{aligned} &= 160 \times 1.3 \\ &= 80 \times 3.1 \\ &= 80 \times 3.9 \\ &= 768 \ (m.kg) \end{aligned}$$

The proa

The classical South Seas proa has a pointed bow and stern rather like a Venetian gondola; it may be symmetrical or asymmetrical. The outrigger is always kept to windward; if it begins to lift, first one man scrambles onto the outrigger, then another, and so on. The boat does not tack in the conventional sense. In practice, it is sailed backwards on the same tack by swinging the sail through 180° and simply shifting the steering oar to the end that is now the stern. For obvious reasons, proas have been unable to compete successfully on triangular courses, but things appear a little different in long-distance events, such as the transatlantic race. *Cheers* is representative of the classical Polynesian proa (see photograph); this vessel from the board of the American designer Dick Newick took a creditable third place in the 1968 OSTAR single-handed transatlantic race against competition from considerably larger yachts.

With 'modern' proas, the cumbersome process of shunting is avoided by having the outrigger either to windward or to leeward, depending on the tack. Let us take a closer look at this more modern version of the proa.

When the proa is sailing with the outrigger to windward, wind pressure overcomes the righting moment if the outrigger lifts out of the water. If the crew is already sitting on the outrigger, the vessel has reached its maximum sail-carrying ability and hence its highest potential speed. The righting moment could be increased only by making the outrigger heavier (and bigger), which would have an adverse effect on total weight. The ultimate form would then be a boat with an outrigger of the same size as the main hull, which would give us a catamaran with the mast stepped on the lee hull!

Let us now go about onto the other tack and sail with the outrigger to leeward. The sail-carrying limit is reached when the outrigger is forced under water. This too could easily be corrected by increasing the volume of the outrigger until it was the same size as the main hull, ending up with a catamaran with the mast on the windward hull!

As a matter of interest, and contrary to widespread belief, it is completely immaterial from the point of view of physics, whether the mast is stepped amidships, to windward or to leeward.

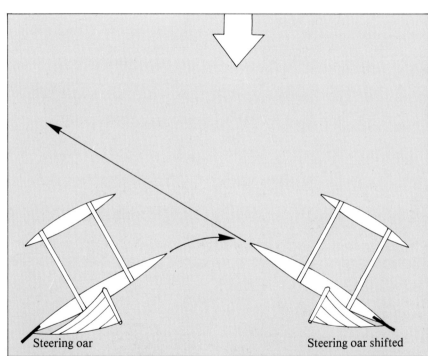

Steering oar · Steering oar shifted

The traditional proa tacks by shunting so that the outrigger always remains to windward. The sail is simply swung through 180° on the leeward side.

Up to now, the proa Cheers *sailed by the American Tom Follett is the only boat of this type to make its mark on the offshore racing scene. In the 1968 OSTAR single-handed transatlantic race it won a surprising third place. In general, however, proas have not gained a wide following, despite the impressive speeds they can reach. Windward capsizes as a result of wave action or inattention on the part of the skipper have proved to be the main problem with boats of this type and have caused all too many competitors to retire.*

The trimaran

It is perfectly correct to regard the trimaran in the same way as the proa; in simplified terms, a trimaran is simply a proa with an additional outrigger that further increases the righting moment. In terms of physics, a trimaran would in fact be a comparable alternative to a catamaran of the same beam.

In practice, however, this does not prove to be the case, for to keep pace with a catamaran of the same length a trimaran must generally have about 30% more beam and be almost 20% heavier than the cat.

In addition, trimarans are more sluggish in a seaway than comparable cats and more problematic in a blow.

That is therefore a further reason why there will be no sports trimarans; the Krakens and Supernovas will not only fail to catch on, they will disappear from the scene.

Catamarans –
as old as seafaring itself

When the Polynesians were sailing the vast expanse of the Pacific, when the forefathers of the Maoris set sail from Polynesia and discovered New Zealand and when Hawaii was being colonised, only a handful of very courageous Europeans would risk sailing out of sight of land in their diminutive and barely seaworthy craft. At that time, when seafaring was still in its infancy, scholars held that those who ventured too far across the ocean were in danger of 'falling off the edge of the world'.

The Polynesians certainly did not regard a voyage of thousands of miles as child's play either, but nor they did consider it an incalculable risk, as in the European culture. If the worst came to the worst, some of the crew would have to be eaten if the ship's livestock ran out.

The first known European multihull was *Invention I*, a twin-hulled boat designed by the Dublin doctor Sir William Petty in 1662. Petty even gained the patronage of King Charles II. It is not known whether he was inspired by the first sketchy reports of this type of craft brought back to Europe by the Dutch explorer Abel Tasman, who discovered New Zealand, Tonga and Fiji in the middle of the seventeenth century.

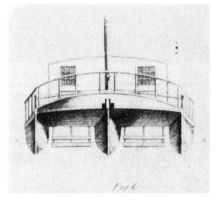

A trimaran built in 1786 by the Scot, Patrick Miller.

When Petty's third twin-hulled boat sank, interest in ships of this kind again subsided without any of the designers realising that the secret of success lay in light construction.

Another partially successful attempt was made by the Scottish businessman Patrick Miller, who built several two- and three-hulled boats from 1786 onwards (illustration, above). These were praised by many contemporaries for their shallow draft and perfectly respectable speeds, but in the long run these too failed to catch on.

It was not until 1876 that the design breakthrough was made by the 'wizard of Bristol', the American Nathaniel Herreshoff: his *Amaryllis* (illustration, right), a 7.60 metre (25 foot) twin-hulled boat of thoroughly modern conception, so outclassed the fleet of the New York Yacht Club that such ships were completely prohibited from any further participation in club regattas. Yet another opportunity to develop catamarans had been wasted.

It is interesting to note the characteristics of catamaran construction that Herreshoff regarded as important even then. 'The catamaran', he wrote 'should always be left in its pure form. It is a light, airy machine that scuds across the water. If one tries to burden it with a cabin all this lightness is lost, and I am sure that such a vessel would be unsatisfactory in every respect.'

The Russian, Victor Tchetchet suffered the same fate as Herreshoff after winning a race at the Kiev Imperial Yacht Club in 1909 in his home-built catamaran – he was banned from competing in further regattas, for what he was sailing was 'not a ship'.

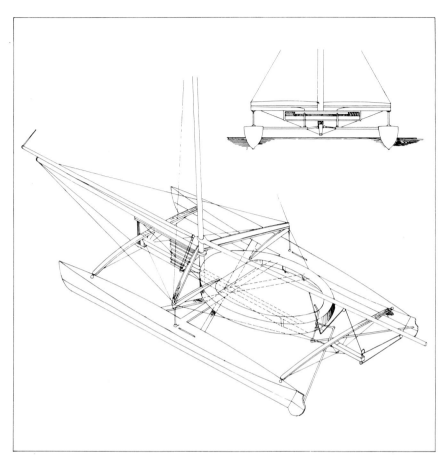

Light construction provided the breakthrough

Amaryllis, designed by the American Nathaniel Herreshoff, was the first catamaran deliberately geared towards light construction.

In Europe, the kudos of being the 'pioneers' in the catamaran field belongs to the English brothers Roland and Francis Prout (photograph), who were champion canoeists and members of the British Olympic team. In the words of Roland, they 'just wanted to see what would happen if we lashed two canoes together and set a rig on them'. Despite its faults, this light vessel proved so fast in trials that the Prouts caught the catamaran bug, thought more deeply about the design and

A further milestone for multihull boats was undoubtedly the voyage by the Frenchmen Eric de Bisschop and Joseph Tatibouet from Hawaii round the Cape of Good Hope to Cannes in 1937 and 1938. Sailing the 13.70 metre (50 foot) catamaran *Kaimiloa* that they had built themselves, they encountered practically no problems on the fourteen-month voyage and proved that multihulls are perfectly capable of making oceanic passages, though the majority of sailors took little notice.

The brothers Roland and Francis Prout were the first Europeans to develop a catamaran to the series production stage. Their design, the Shearwater III, is still one of the most active racing classes in the United Kingdom.

unveiled the first prototype of the
famous Shearwater in 1954. The first
British Championship of the Shearwater
II (see photograph on page 14) was held
as early as 1957; over the years this boat
has been greatly modified, but it is still
one of the largest catamaran classes in
the United Kingdom.

When Prince Philip sailed a Shearwater prototype in 1954, the cat became
socially respectable; the fast twin-hulled
boats finally became part of the sailing
establishment when the International
Yacht Racing Union (IYRU) set up its
Multihull Committe in 1959.

Britain remained the stronghold of
catamaran sailing in Europe. Cat fever
spread to the continent of Europe – the
'Deutsche Cat Club' was founded in
1957 – and even the Russians became
active (see illustration right), but the
further development of the catamaran is
inseparable from names such as Prout
(Shearwater), Mazzotti (Mantua, Unicorn), Macalpine-Downie (Hellcat,
Shark) and Rodney March (Tornado,
Dart), to name but a few.

At an early stage the IYRU recognised the need to subdivide the range of
catamarans and created the A, B, C and
D Classes, though this was intended to
be no more than a guide.

In 1967 the Tornado (see page 17)
emerged from the IYRU's comparative
trials in the Thames estuary as *the* B

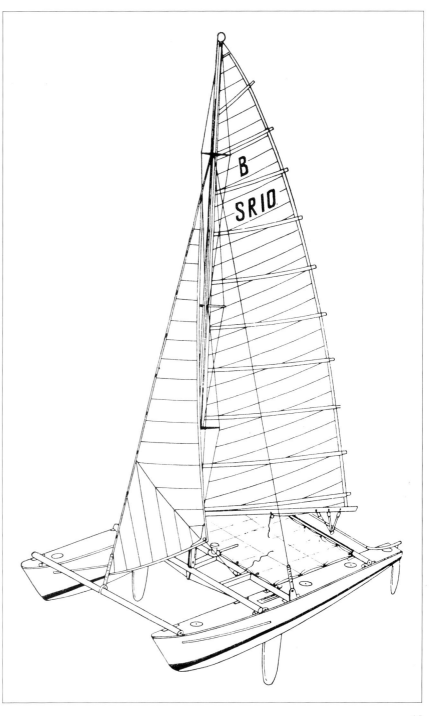

◀ *The Shearwater III in action, as it looks after
almost 25 years of development. For many
years it was the only catamaran to set a
spinnaker but recently other classes have
adopted the sail.*

In 1963 and 1964 the Russians Romanov and ▶
*Alexeyev designed a B Class catamaran that
is thoroughly modern even by today's
standards and which proved extremely fast in
regattas off Leningrad.*

The IYRU Catamaran Classes		
A Class	Length overall (excluding rudders) Beam overall Sail area, including mast and boom* Single-handed class	max. 5.48 m(17.9 ft) max. 2.30 m(7.5 ft) max.13.94 sq m(150.0 sq ft)
B Class	Length overall (excluding rudders) Beam overall Sail area, including mast and boom* Two-man class	max. 6.09 m(19.9 ft) max. 3.05 m(10.0 ft) max.21.83 sq m(234.9 sq ft)
C Class	Length overall (excluding rudders) Beam overall Sail area, including mast and boom* Two-man class	max. 7.62 m(24.9 ft) max. 4.27 m(14.0 ft) max.27.80 sq m(299.2 sq ft)
D Class	Length overall (excluding rudders) Beam overall Sail area, including mast and boom* Three-man class	unrestricted unrestricted max.46.40 sq m(499.4 sq ft)

*As catamarans usually have rotating masts, the mast and boom present an appreciable additional area to the wind and are therefore included in the total sail area. In the Wing (A Class), for example, the mast and boom constitute more than 10% of the total sail area.

Class catamaran; when this class became the first catamaran to gain Olympic status in 1976, the great boom began. Catamaran classes sprang from boatyards like the proverbial mushrooms, and buyers became increasingly confused as the doctrinal war reached its peak among designers and others who claimed the title.

Design and development work had proceeded apace in the A Class since its inception; this was important for the development of catamarans as a whole, but not particularly beneficial to the A Class itself. For years Class A in Europe was dominated by two types of boat: the Unicorn, designed by the Englishman John Mazzotti, and the Wing, from the board of the German Klaus J Enzmann. In recent years, however, fast designs from Italy have been making a name for themselves, such as the Bim by Michelangelo Petrucci and the O.K. by Corrado Sirri.

Italian designs came on the scene fairly late. The fact that catamarans are now a recognised class of boat there too, is due in no small measure to the Vele di Pasqua regatta in Cesenatico, which is held exclusively for catamarans.

The Australians and Americans, who have tackled Class A rather more systematically in recent years, are also now a force to be reckoned with. The debate whether to become a one-design class and whether to restrict the mast height is exercising the minds of sailors and class officials alike; if Class A can survive these tensions, as is to be hoped, the results should be interesting.

There is active racing in Classes A and B, which therefore have a wide following. C Class catamarans occasionally earn a mention in the press, such as at the time of the races for the Little America's Cup. Only Class D has been slumbering for years. Was the IYRU class division wrong? We do not think so. D Class catamarans are uniquely suited to help establish a class of boats so aptly described as camper cruisers; up to now, however, the idea does not seem to have occurred to designers . . .

Besides progress in the IYRU Classes, there have naturally been very lively developments in other directions – on the one hand towards racing classes that do not fall into the IYRU categories and on the other towards pure 'pleasure boats', though the latter should by no means be regarded as inferior boats. A prime example of the latter type of boat is the Hobie, which has been on the market for more than ten years and is now the most widespread class in the world; according to the international class association, almost 100,000 boats have been sold and the association has a membership of around 65,000. It would be difficult to imagine a more rapid transformation from pure pleasure boat to active racing class.

The Californian Hubert 'Hobie' Alter, the 'inventor' of this type of boat, probably never imagined where it would lead when he developed a simple boat just for the fun of sailing; there are now three versions – the Hobie 14 (illustrated on page 20), the Hobie 16 and the Hobie 18. It is hardly surprising that many designers have tried to emulate him, though none has even come near to matching his success.

Nevertheless, in designing this type of boat Hubert Alter initiated a development that has still a long way to go. And who can say whether sailing just for fun is not the better way?

Reg White sailed the Tornado to victory in the IYRU selection trials in 1967 and won the Olympic gold medal in this class in 1976. He is still sailing competitively; the photograph shows him sailing perfectly during the 1982 Tornado European Championship on Lake Garda.

In 1980 the Americans Steve Edmonds and Bill Roberts brought out the Supercat. This was the first of the modern designs to be able to shake the Tornado's reputation as the fastest catamaran. The Supercat remains easy to transport, thanks to its telescopic crossbeams.

The 18m² Class is particularly widespread in the USA. Since it is a development class, designers have considerable latitude. Like the A Class catamarans, this design has enlivened the entire catamaran scene. The photograh shows a Nacra 5.2 modified to qualify for the 18m² class.

The G-Cat, designed in the USA in 1976 by
Horst Geissler, has built up a reputation as a
robust all-rounder. A larger brother, the
G-Cat 18, followed in 1981. Both are suitable
as family boats, for with a tent over the
forward trampoline the G-Cat can be used
for cruising.

Like the Hobie, the Prindle is based on
asymmetrical hulls. Small wonder, since the
designer, Geoffrey Prindle, worked with
'Hobie' Alter in California. Designed in
1972, the Prindle now ranks as one of the
most popular classes in the catamaran world
after the Hobies.

The Hobie 14 designed by the Californian 'Hobie' Alter is simple in concept and carries the minimum by way of trimming aids. As it manages to do without a centreboard, it can be beached. The Hobie was originally intended as a pure funboat, but owners quickly developed racing ambitions, so that it is now one of the most actively raced catamaran classes. The simple design concept remains essentially unchanged.

Catamarans – a diverse family

Given the Polynesian and European parentage of the modern catamaran, it should come as no surprise that its numerous offspring differ widely in style and temperament. Nowadays the aspiring catamaran sailor has an awesome choice, ranging from the staid to the exotic, from the robust funboat to the hypersensitive racing machine.

Regrettably, manufacturers and dealers are still assailing buyers with arguments from the 'doctrinal war' between the various design principles, which on the whole cannot make the decision any easier. This behaviour, which has even filtered through to some of the class associations, is anything but helpful to those wishing to take up multihull sailing or to switch from a monohull. In fact, all the different boat

concepts are essentially mature and well suited to their respective purposes.

In the final anaylsis, there will inevitably be a wide range of designs and concepts, for certain design options will be mutually exclusive, depending on the intended purpose of the boat, funboat or racing machine. Every vessel is ultimately a compromise, and catamarans are no exception; the buyer must decide what is important for him and for the way in which he intends to use the boat. The following chapter should help him decide.

Concepts and classes

Two hulls are better than one...

...that far, at least, we are on firm ground – despite the protestations of the monohull camp, which we shall ignore for the time being, However, the next stage is already rather more complicated: Which material is preferable? What are the advantages of the different building methods? Should a cat have a centreboard or not? Which hull shape is preferable?

Let us first look at building materials. Unquestionably, glass reinforced plastic (GRP) is by far the most widely used material in the construction of catamarans today. Wood is still quite common, but it is used almost exclusively for pure racing machines – which says a lot for wood.

GRP is almost completely immune to rot, it is strong and easy to maintain,

though not entirely maintenance-free. It also lends itself to series manufacture, a fact that is of greater interest to the producer than to the boat owner. Nevertheless, most GRP repairs can be done at home, an advantage that should not be underestimted at today's prices.

The main disadvantages of GRP construction are the material's relatively high weight and low panel stiffness, which must be offset by reinforcements, mainly in the form of ribs or stringers. This leads to a further increase in weight, which in turn requires even stronger joints and brings still more weight – a vicious circle that only good designers and boatyards are able to break.

Building in GRP sandwich still has a rather exotic reputation. As a rule, it is only used for racing catamarans at present. Various materials may be used for the core. Traditionally, end-grain balsa wood has been used, but a whole range of man-made materials is now available, such as honeycomb, foam, granular fillers and Coremat (diagram, page 22); the latter often has fine perforations to ensure a firm bond with the laminates on either side. Hulls in sandwich construction are as easy to maintain as

normal GRP hulls, but they are considerably lighter and stiffer – an ideal building method then? Well no, for this system also has its disadvantages. First, the materials used must be a very precise chemical match to ensure a permanent bond. Secondly, the hulls are more vulnerable to loads concentrated at a point and once water has penetrated the sandwich (as a result of a collision, for example) it is almost impossible to get it out. In addition, construction and repair are much more complicated than in the case of a normal GRP boat.

With sandwich construction, the position of fittings must also be planned well in advance, as the laminate must have no sandwich layer at the chosen spot. It is therefore extremely difficult for the layman to mount fittings elsewhere at a later date.

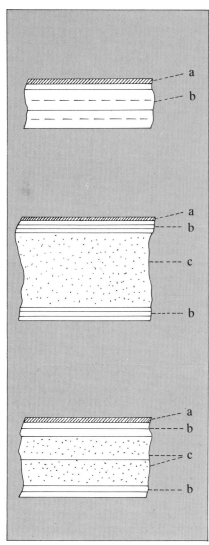

Top. GRP construction. a = outer gelcoat layer, 0.3 mm–1.0 mm (0.01 in–0.03 in); b = GRP laminate from chopped strand mat and woven roving.

Middle. Sandwich construction. a = outer gelcoat layer, 0.3 mm–1.0 mm (0.01 in–0.03 in); b = GRP laminate from chopped strand mat or woven roving; c = core consisting of foam, balsa wood or a mixture of resin and glass microspheres.

Bottom. Coremat sandwich: a = outer gelcoat layer, 0.3 mm–1.0 mm (0.01 in–0.03 in); b = GRP laminate from chopped strand mat or woven roving; c = Coremat.

The quickest and cheapest way of building a catamaran hull is to use the stitch and glue method. Two symmetrical sheets of plywood are stitched together along the keel with copper wire and then opened out wide enough to produce the final angle at the keel. The keel is then laminated on both sides with epoxy resin and woven glassfibre (above left). After being well dampened (above right), the sheets are bent together and pressed into a prepared jig (lower right). Illustrated here is the construction of a Tornado in the yard of Herbert Glas, probably the most experienced builder using this method.

Wood is still wood

The history of seafaring began with wood; thanks to modern glues, which made the development of waterproof marine plywood possible, wood has again become a popular building material, particularly for home construction and racing boats.

If buyers were to weigh up the advantages and disadvantages of wood, the result should come out more or less evenly balanced. Surprisingly enough, that is not the case in reality! The main reason why the majority of buyers shy away from a wooden boat is probably that it requires more maintenance than a pure GRP hull, even if it is built using modern methods, such as the WEST System. (WEST is the registered trade mark of the Wood Epoxy Saturation Technique, developed for use in series production by the American Gougeon brothers.)

It is interesting to compare a wooden

boat with one in sandwich construction.

Wood is unsurpassed for its lightness and the high panel stiffness that can be achieved. Moreover, wood is ideally suited for amateur construction, particularly the building of catamarans, a fact that probably often tips the scales in its favour. The amateur does not need to spend time building expensive moulds, for by preference he will use the stitch and glue method (see illustrations), which has been widely used for years in the construction of Tornados, Unicorns and other catamarans. Cold moulded hulls disappeared from the catamaran scene long ago; the cost had simply become prohibitive.

The hull – a load-bearing member

Anyone interested in acquiring a catamaran should look closely at the load-bearing capacity of the hulls as well the material from which they are built. Nathaniel Herreshoff already noted that excessive weight was bad. Even an overweight crew can transform a lively small catamaran into a sluggish and unstable craft (see illustration on page 24). Whether father sails the catamaran alone or can take along his son, wife, daughter or grandmother depends on the displacement for which the hulls have been designed. For that reason, even two single-handers of different weights will choose different types of

Three fully grown men are simply too much for a fairly small catamaran. The effect is plain from the photograph: the boat is too low in the water and is making a clearly visible wave; the strain on fittings and on the rig is enormous in anything of a wind. The greater weight on the windward gunwale does not make the catamaran any safer, in fact it gives the boat a tendency to bury its bows and makes its motions sluggish.

boat if they want to win races. Prospective purchasers would therefore be well advised to ask the salesman or class association for the maximum designed displacement, though many of the slicker salesmen may squirm a little.

But even if you sail purely for pleasure you should not wantonly overload your cat, for you will pay the price not only in terms of a drop in boat speed and a much wetter sail but also in unusual sluggishness and faster wear and tear.

It is also advisable to bear in mind the particular characteristics of the area in which you intend to sail: in predominantly choppy waters, every extra centimetre of freeboard means drier sailing.

The centreboard question

In the pure racing classes A, B, C and D supervised by the IYRU, the centreboard is not an issue: it must be there. In other equally active classes, however, the debate whether to have a board or not is far from closed and will probably continue for many years to come.

There are two essential points in favour of having a centreboard: a cat with a centreboard points much better than one without and the scope for trimming is far wider. Two further plus points are a bonus: first, when it is blowing so hard that safety becomes the first priority, the leeward board can be raised so that the lee hull can slide away

more easily in a squall, thereby preventing a capsize, and secondly a centreboard projecting from a hull provides useful leverage if the boat has to be righted.

An easy decision, then? No, because centreboards also have a number of disadvantages. First, they are highly vulnerable to damage in the water and on land. Secondly, the catamaran sailor already has two rudders to contend with; the crew of a cat with centreboards must therefore also worry about the boards. Finally, the design is more complicated, as two centreboard cases must be built and supported (and of course made watertight) – in the final analysis, they are features that cost money and must be paid for, obviously by the purchaser.

It is still not plain sailing once one has decided on a centreboard boat, for the

Despite its great hydrodynamic efficiency, the daggerboard has not caught on. Not only is the board a problem close to shore, but a partly or wholly raised board considerably hampers the actions of the crew.

The pivoted centreboard offers greater scope for trimming the boat – the photographs show a Tornado board half lowered and fully extended – but has a poorer hydrodynamic performance.

next question concerns the type of board. Normally the choice is between the daggerboard and the pivoted centreboard, but it is not easy to decide between the two.

Unquestionably, the daggerboard is hydrodynamically more effective than the pivoted centreboard. It is also easier and cheaper to build and lighter in weight. These advantages, which should not be underestimated, are balanced by a number of disadvantages (everything is a compromise!). If you run aground with a daggerboard, it is almost inevitable that the board will be damaged, and often the hull too; if the board is raised, it almost invariably impedes the actions of the crew, particularly on smaller cats.

By contrast, the pivoted centreboard (illustrated) is easy to raise, remains out of sight in the centreboard case and usually lifts of its own accord without danger of breaking if you run aground. It also offers greater trim possibilities, as the centre of lateral resistance can be moved aft. The disadvantages are greater design effort, higher construction cost, higher weight and greater space requirement. The main drawback with pivoted centreboards is that they can never have the hydrodynamic efficiency of a daggerboard. Partially raising the pivoted board gives it a less streamlined profile (diagram left). In addition, the problem of sealing the part of the centreboard case not closed by the board has still not been fully resolved.

Wood (laminated or solid), GRP (generally a foam core with a GRP sheathing) and aluminium (hollow or foam filled) have proved suitable materials for centreboards.

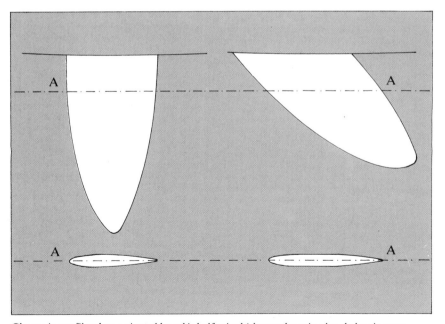

Change in profile when a pivoted board is half raised (shown above in plan, below in cross-section); A = plane of the cross-section.

Better without a centreboard?

Those who claim that centreboards are old hat argue that the ancient Polynesians sailed without them. However, this assertion is not quite correct; on many Polynesian double canoes the paddles were slotted into brackets along the side of the hull when sailing to windward, so that they not only helped trim the boat but also acted as effective lateral resistance.

Nevertheless, the arguments advanced by the 'no-board faction' of catamaran designers are impressive:

Hulls without centreboards are lighter and obviously easier to build, which in turn should be reflected in a lower price. Furthermore, colliding with flotsam or sailing up the beach present no problems or risk of damage. The sailor also has less to do, for he does not have to bother about uphauls and downhauls, tripping devices and the like, and has fewer loose ends around the boat.

But where there is sun there is also shadow. The shadow takes the form of poorer pointing ability, limited scope for trimming and the fact that in a blow the boat cannot be made to slide to leeward under control.

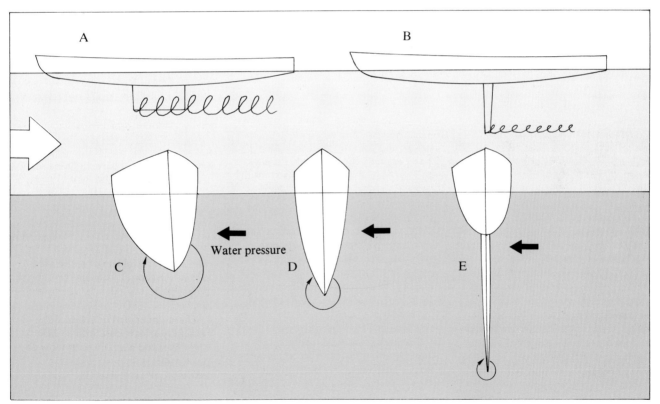

Induced resistance is generated at the ends of a body immersed in a moving fluid. It takes the form of a vortex created by the air or water attempting to flow round the end of the foil from the low pressure side to the high pressure side.
A. long shallow keel = high induced resistance
B. deep narrow keel = low induced resistance
C. asymmetrical hull form = high induced resistance
D. symmetrical deep V hull form = better
E. centreboard best

Symmetrical or asymmetrical?

Our friends in the Hobie and Prindle camps will not like to hear this, but asymmetrical hulls do not offer any appreciable advantages.

This had been proved not least by extensive tank tests carried out by the Massachusetts Institute of Technology into induced resistance at the end of profiles (diagram, page 27) and the theoretical and practical studies made by Rodney March before designing the Dart. Even the American, Rudy Choy, one of the most experienced catamaran designers in the world, has now moved away from the asymmetrical form; his latest racing catamaran, the Machete, has symmetrical hulls fitted with centreboards.

There are two main arguments against asymmetrical hulls. The first is basic design: the vortex generated at the lower edge of the hulls causes more resistance than with any other hull form. The second reason is economic: two moulds must be built for a cat with asymmetrical hulls, which is only worthwhile for long production runs, as in the case of the Hobies and Prindles.

The lift to windward that the asymmetrical lee hull is generally supposed to generate only occurs if the windward hull has lifted completely out of the water; in all earlier stages the shape of the windward hull generates lift to leeward, thereby cancelling out the desired effect produced by the lee hull. In any case, it is debatable whether the lee hull can generate lift in choppy conditions. On top of this there is the higher induced resistance.

Be that as it may, we believe that arguments about symmetry versus asymmetry get us nowhere. Let us therefore let the Hobies, Prindles and other asymmetrical cats have their asymmetry; after all, the boats in these classes are identical, so that no-one suffers any disadvantages – and they do have the benefit of a boardless hull.

A rudderless cat?

The rudderless cat actually exists; it is the Spanish *patin a vela,* which translates more or less as 'sailing skate'. The helmsman steers solely by shifting his weight and working hard with the sheet. This design by the Spaniards Lasaosa and the Monge brothers is an exception, however, although in the sixy years since it was launched it has become a very popular class in Spain.

'Normal' catamarans cannot dispense with a rudder. Surprisingly enough, skippers rarely discuss the design of rudders, in contrast to the centreboard issue. This is difficult to understand, as from the hydrodynamic point of view the rudder is certainly no less important or interesting than the centreboard.

The lifting rudder is currently the most common form. Its advantages lie in its simple design, the ever important safety in the event of grounding (for the blade can swivel upwards) and the general ease of use, since in almost all catamarans on the market today the rudder blades can be raised and lowered by lever action on the tiller. However,

Since the rudder blades of the Topcat (a continental class of 4.8 metres (15.7 feet)) can be raised vertically when close to the beach (top), the rudder's centre of resistance and the rudder pressure do not change when the blade is raised. In the event of accidental grounding, the blade nevertheless pivots backwards like a conventional rudder (bottom).

lifting rudders have one serious drawback: they are very difficult to tune precisely, for they must have a certain minimum play.

In the case of the daggerplate rudder, on the other hand, it is easier to tune the rudder blade to the hull because control can be much more precise. Even when it is not fully lowered, the daggerplate rudder is not subject to the extreme rudder loads that occur with partly raised kick-up rudders. Nevertheless, this type of rudder is not as ideal as it sounds, for it is rather difficult to fix a device that will release in the event of grounding.

From a technical point of view, one system (illustrated left) points in the right direction, but only large production runs make economical sense.

Many catamaran classes are now using semi-balanced rudders, the operation of which can be seen clearly in the diagram, which also shows the fully balanced rudder and the simple transom-hung variety. The latter are commonplace, but fully balanced rudders are extremely rare. In the case of the semi-balanced rudder, the lack of rudder pressure is both an advantage and a disadvantage. In the final analysis, rudder pressure simply

indicates that something is wrong with the trim of the vessel. Without the feel transmitted by the rudder, a helmsman who is not extremely attentive may not realise that the boat is wrongly trimmed; if he is racing, he will then wonder why he is at the back of the fleet.

Apart from giving thought to the shape and size of the catamaran's rudder, you should also pay frequent attention to the kick-up mechanism. Too slack a setting may cost you victory in a race if the blades suddenly release of their own accord; on the other hand, if they do not release when they should, it could cost you a new transom.

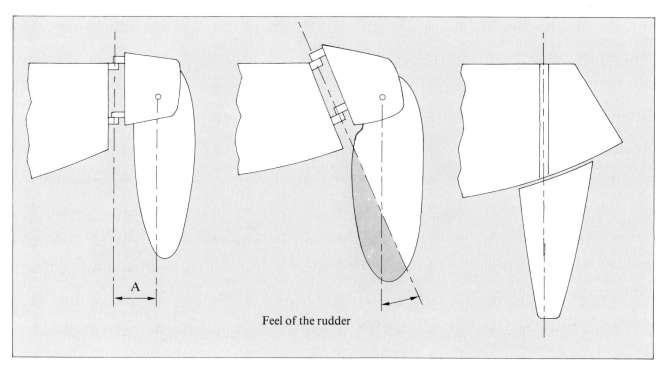

Feel of the rudder

Transom-hung rudder (large distance A between the axis of the rudder and its centre of effort):
+ high degree of feel
+ low loading
+ high sculling effect
− heavy rudder pressure
(A Class cats, Topcat)

Semi-balanced rudder (the smaller part of the blade surface is in front of the axis, the larger behind it):
± average feel
− higher loading
± lower sculling effect
+ lower rudder pressure
(Tornado, Dart, Hobie)

Fully balanced rudder (the rudder axis and the centre of effort of the blade pass through the same point):
− no feel
− high loading
− no sculling effect
+ no rudder pressure
(O.K., many cruising catamarans)

A power catamaran?

We do not intend to present a motorised catamaran here. The power source of your cat is of course the sails and the rig on which they are set.

As a rule, a catamaran moves much faster through air and water than a monohull. For that reason the catamaran sailor should come to terms with aerodynamics and hydrodynamics in greater detail than would otherwise be the case. The standard work by C A Marchaj, *Aero-Hydrodynamics of Sailing*, (Adlard Coles, 1979), leaves no question unanswered, but calls for a prior knowledge of physics and careful study.

It is true to say that the entire catamaran rig must be able to withstand and convert much greater forces than that of a monohull. If we assume that in a 10-knot wind the force applied to the rig of a monohull yacht is 100%, the loading on a multihull is as much as 160% simply as a result of the higher speed (diagram below).

It is little wonder, therefore, that the shrouds and stays on catamarans appear to be oversize. Current practice is to attach the shrouds and forestay at a single point on the forward side of the mast (see photograph). The mast is then free to rotate behind this attachment,

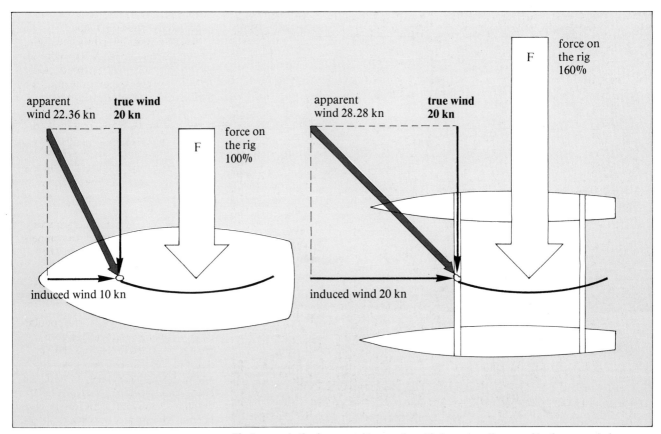

The increase in the forces working on rigs with the same sail area and in the same wind strength solely as a result of the increase in the induced wind: left a dinghy, right a catamaran (simplified calculation of the apparent wind).

Shrouds, forestay, trapeze wire and nowadays often diamond stays as well, are led to a single main anchorage so that the mast can turn easily about its longitudinal axis. In the Topcat this is simply a hook on which is hung a ring attached to all the standing rigging (foreground), while the Tornado has a robust stainless steel fitting to which the wire rigging is shackled (background).

thereby greatly helping to produce a good aerodynamic sail shape.

Rotating masts are now standard in almost all catamarans. Mast sections should be as long and narrow as possible, and in many classes the mast is further stiffened athwartships by diamond struts. As the diagrams on page 32 show, the ideal solution would be a rigid wingsail, as it has the best aerodynamic characteristics. However, no designer has yet managed to solve all the problems that this type of rig entails.

Wingsails have been used experimentally and almost exclusively on C-Class catamarans which compete for The Little America's Cup. They have been allowed since 1982.

The rotating mast with a battened sail will therefore probably remain the norm for some time to come. ·

Where class rules allow, the popular pear-shaped mast section has been greatly elongated in the fore and aft direction but slimmed down in width and is moving increasingly towards the aerodynamic ideal. This development depends to no small degree on the cost of the necessary aerodynamic trials and materials tests. The future will see small and cautious steps towards aerodynamic improvements.

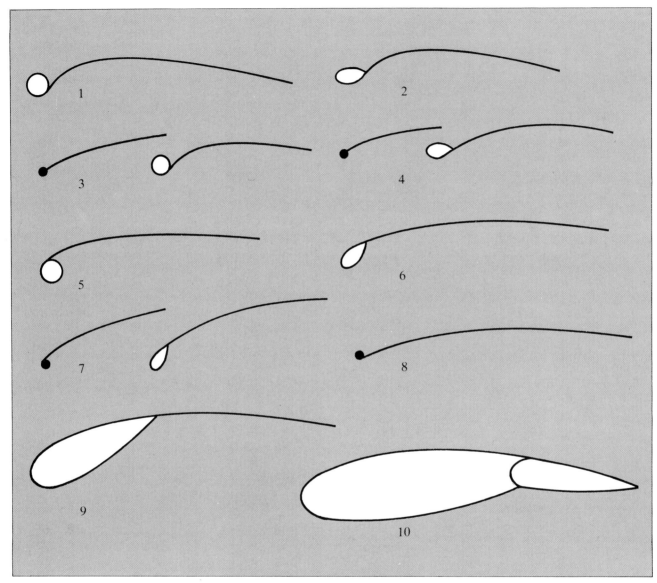

A comparison of the efficiency of the various rig profiles and leading edges (assuming equal sail areas and battened sails)
1. round mast, non-rotating = 63%
2. shaped mast, non-rotating = 65%
3. round mast, non-rotating, with jib = 71%
4. shaped mast, non-rotating, with jib = 73%
5. round mast, rotating, with or without jib = 78%
6. shaped mast, rotating, without jib = 82%
7. shaped mast, rotating, with jib = 83%
8. foresail alone = 83%
9. airfoil mast, width 30%–40% of section length = 94%
10. rigid airfoil with flaps = **100%**

For the same sail area, a rig with a boom allows the centre of effort of the sail to be lowered from S to S₁.

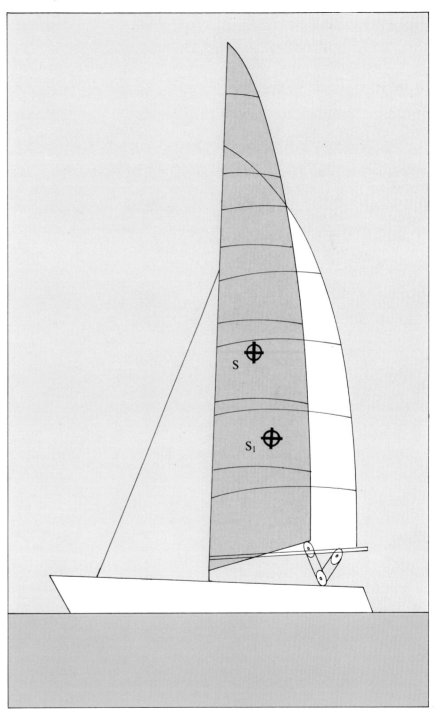

The boom: reefing aid or guillotine?

It comes as no surprise that the early catamarans were equipped with a boom, for that was the norm in traditional boatbuilding. Moreover, as the sailors first had to learn how to handle these fast boats, it was initially a question of keeping the centre of effort of the sail as low as possible, not a good thing in terms of aerodynamics but better from the point of view of handling and safety (diagram right). If the class rules allow, a designer can now draw the same sail area on a taller rig, so that the clew automatically moves forward, thereby creating the necessary sheeting angle, that is to say forwards and upwards.

The boomless mainsail has become popular, particularly among the more modern fun catamarans; the reduction in the risk of injury fully compensates for the rather poorer adjustment of the foot of the sail. The racing classes will probably not dispense with the boom quite so quickly, although there are now A Class catamarans that have proved fully competitive with a boomless sail (see photograph overleaf).

The boom offers one advantage that even its opponents cannot gainsay: only a mainsail set on a boom can be reefed, as in the Hobie, which was originally designed for an area of strong winds. If the designer makes provision for a boom, he should definitely specify a

loose foot, for only in this way can small adjustments to the sail be made effectively.

Nowadays, a cutaway foot has found favour as a way of reducing the considerable induced resistance in that area (diagram below).

The first proponent of boomless catamarans within the racing classes was the O.K. Even without a boom, this boat proved fully competitive.

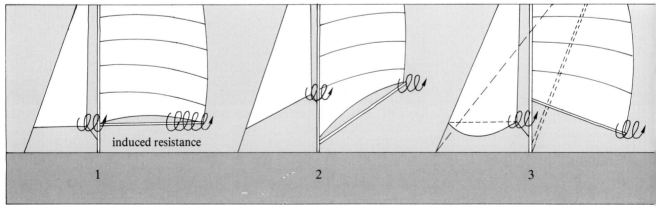

Bad.
horizontal, long and open foot; in this instance, it would be better if it were attached to the boom.

Better.
shorter foot, angled upwards and set loose or: foot of jib rounded, with camber sewn into the sail.

or: boom angled downwards, with the foot attached to the boom or: a combination of 2 and 3.

Forward march of the stiff rig

Stiff rig or flexible rig? The debate on this issue is still not closed. A mast is described as stiff if it has little or no bend both fore and aft and athwartships (see diagram right).

Mast section axes (masts are normally considerably stiffer in the x axis than in the y axis).
Section 1 (Unicorn = A Class): extremely flexible in both x and y axes.
Section 2 (Tornado, Topcat, Dart): normal flexibility and in widespread use.
Section 3 (Wing = A Class): almost rigid in the x axis with normal flexibility in the y axis.

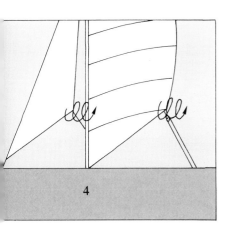

Best.
tall, narrow sails with a short, upward angled foot, boomless mainsail.

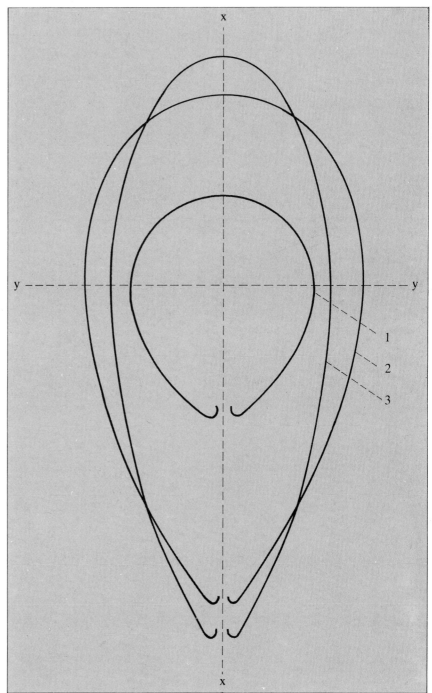

There are two important reasons why stiff masts will continue to gain ground. First, the sail is easier to trim, as the depth and shape of the sail camber are regulated solely by luff tension, clew outhaul, batten tension and sheet tension. Secondly, the aerodynamic efficiency of modern rigs is already so good that it could only be surpassed by a rigid wing mast with flaps or sails attached to its trailing edge (see the diagram on page 32). Since a stiff mast allows the desired motive force to be achieved without a jib, the designer can dispense with the foresail without sacrificing much performance.

Despite its many advantages, the stiff rig also exhibits a number of disadvantages that have hitherto impeded its eventual triumph. Masts with the required stiffness and aerodynamic shape are significantly heavier than flexible masts of much smaller section. The greater weight aloft accentuates pitching and rolling by increasing the boat's moment of inertia. Moreover, rigid masts (section depths from front to back of up to about 150 mm (6 in) are common, as sections such as this can

During the 1974 Little America's Cup the Australian Miss Nylex, *with a wingsail of 10.9 m height and a sail area of 27.8 m², beat New Zealand's* Miss Star Travel *with a profile mast and fully battened mainsail. She won by a convincing four to zero margin, but despite its aeorodynamic superiority the rig has lost favour because of its unwieldiness.*

still be extruded from aluminium) are more complicated to build, since as a rule they must also have internal stiffeners, and hence they are more expensive than flexible masts.

Finally, a mast of elongated section provides sail area (see the photographs), and a great many catamarans rigged in this way have capsized on their mooring or on land. The only remedy is to lower the mast immediately the sailing is over – a rather laborious procedure.

The greatest advantage of the flexible rig is that it offers greater scope for trimming the mainsail. By bending the mast, the shape of the sail can be varied considerably, which means that much greater attention must be paid to the match between the mast and the sail. The photographs on the next two pages illustrate the many trim possibilities offered by the flexible rig. However, the greater the scope, the greater the danger of distorting the sail permanently or just for the duration of the race. As flexible rigs never match the aerodynamic performance of rigid rigs, the jib is a sensible addition.

Although profile masts became the norm long ago in C Class, designs such as that of the Swiss Rudi Schmid remain an exception in other racing classes. The photograph shows his Wing with a pronounced aerofoil mast.

Among the more common catamarans, the one with the most flexible rig is at present the Unicorn. The mast is extremely flexible in both directions, with the result that the sails can be cut particularly full (right, top). The sail is first drawn as flat as possible by means of the clew outhaul (right). If that is not enough, mast bend is increased by hauling on the mainsheet and Cunningham hole adjuster until the sail is as flat as a board (right, bottom).

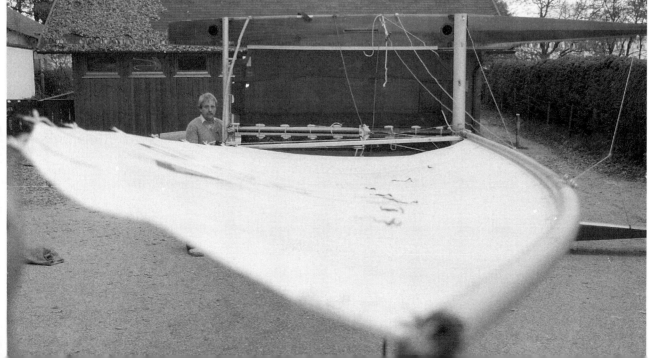

Una rig or sloop rig?

There is really only one thing wrong with a jib: being an additional sail, it requires additional handling, so that the single-handed sailor will gladly dispense with it.

On the other hand, the foresail offers a range of advantages. First, with a jib the same sail area can be achieved with a lower centre of effort, so that the cat becomes stiffer, particularly in the longitudinal axis (see diagram below). At the same time, in a two-man boat each member of the crew has a smaller sail area to handle, so that the strength each requires is less. Far more important, however, is the fact that the jib is a valuable additional sail with a largely unimpeded leading edge, particularly if it has a luff pocket. However, the slot effect generated by the foresail is still overestimated by most catamaran sailors. The effect is such that on courses between about 70° and 140° to the true wind the airflow across the mainsail remains smooth for longer, but it brings hardly any improvement in windward performance, assuming the mainsail is set correctly. It comes into its own off the wind. Particularly when tacking downwind (see pages 84 and 85), a properly setting jib produces a substantial aerodynamic gain (diagram, right). It is therefore incomprehensible that many crews pay their sail the attention it deserves only when sailing to windward.

If the designer has provided for an unbattened jib, it can be set on furling gear, which allows the entire sail area to be reduced quickly and easily, an advantage that undoubtedly appeals to many sailors, and not just those who sail for pleasure.

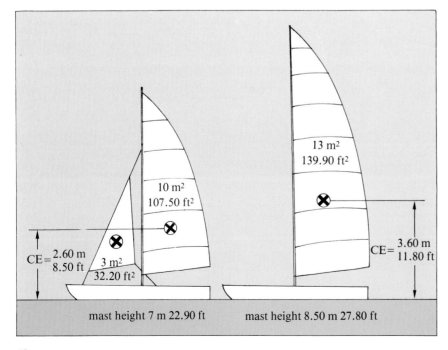

10 m²
107.50 ft²

3 m²
32.20 ft²

CE = 2.60 m
8.50 ft

mast height 7 m 22.90 ft

13 m²
139.90 ft²

CE = 3.60 m
11.80 ft

mast height 8.50 m 27.80 ft

With the same sail area, a jib allows the centre of effort of the sail (CE) to be brought considerably lower.

The trampoline is not for jumping on

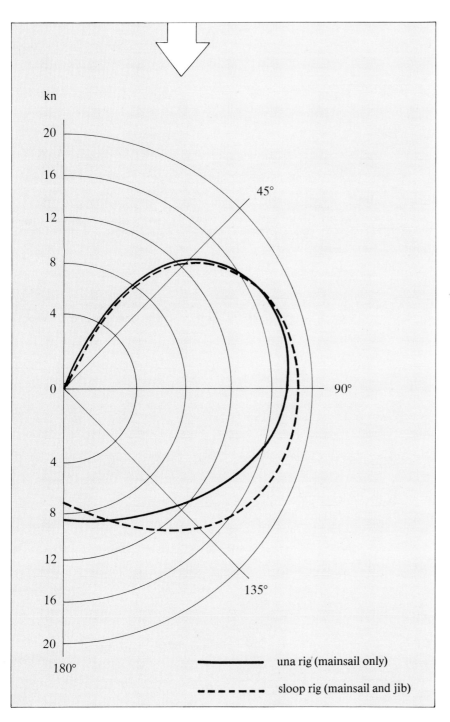

In the early days of the catamaran, rigid fixed decks were the norm, but as designers and boatbuilders learnt to handle the forces developed in a twin-hulled boat it was replaced by a trampoline of cloth or nylon mesh (illustrated on page 42). There are virtually no cats with a fixed deck nowadays; it disappearance can be attributed mainly to its weight and the disadvantages when dismantling the boat.

The disadvantages of the fixed deck are the strong points of the trampoline, and yet it wears out much faster, stubbornly resists efforts to attach fittings, gives the crew a wetter sail and provides no stowage. A trampoline must also be tightened from time to time and the lacing inspected.

Comparison of the lift provided by a una rig and a sloop rig of equal sail area on various courses.

una rig (mainsail only)

sloop rig (mainsail and jib)

Fixed bridgedecks between the hulls, such as those still seen on many older Shearwater catamarans, have long since gone out of fashion, not least on account of their weight.

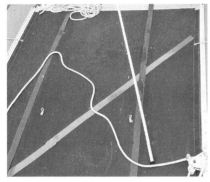

The trampoline between the hulls made it possible to build catamarans light for the first time and to dismantle extra wide boats for transportation. The photograph shows the diagonally cut mesh trampoline on a Stampede. Sewing the mesh or cloth diagonally to the eventual direction of tension ensures that when the trampoline is stretched taut fore and aft it also tightens sideways.

A taut trampoline is not only more streamlined than a slack one, it is also more comfortable and provides a firmer footing. A wise catamaran sailor will therefore check the lacing of the trampoline each time before setting out.

31 catamarans at a glance

	LOA (ft)	Beam (ft)	Sail (sq. ft)	Hull material	Crew	Rig	Club racing	Int. racing	Fun	Other	Int. class	Remarks
Catapult	16.4	7.4	107	Inflatable plastic	1/2	U			•			Inflatable single-handed cat. Can be sailed two-up.
Catapult Comet	16.4	7.4	107	Inflatable plastic	1	U			•			Identical hull to Catapult but with fully battened Mylar sail.
Catapult Cannon	16.4	7.4	107	Inflatable plastic	1	U			•			Identical to Comet but with trapeze.
Condor	16.5	7.6	194	GRP	2	S	•					Fast, two-man racing cat.
Dart	18.0	7.6	172	GRP	2	U	•	•	•		•	Two-man racing cat without centreboards.
G-Cat 5m	16.8	7.8	209	GRP	2	S	•					Two-man racing cat.
G-Cat 5.7m	18.9	7.8	236	GRP	2	S	•					Two-man racing cat.
Hawke Surfcat	13.0	6.2	130	GRP	1/2	U/S	•		•			Tough, Australian-designed fun and beach boat. Can be raced.
Hellcat 12	12.0	7.0	100	GRP	1	S	•		•			Single-handed racing catamaran.
Hellcat 14	14.0	7.4	137	GRP	2	S	•					Two-man racing cat.
Hobie 14	14.0	7.6	118	GRP	1/2	U	•	•	•			Single-hander that can also be sailed two-up. Excellent beach boat.
Hobie 16	16.0	7.9	218	GRP	2	S	•	•	•			Two-man trapeze boat. Strong racing fleets worldwide. Twin wires.
Hobie 17	17.0	8.0	230	GRP	2	U						Hobie 17 not yet in production. Few details known.
Hobie 18	18.0	8.0	240	GRP	2	S	•	•	•			High performance two-man, twin wire racing cat.
Hydra	16.5	7.5	168	GRP	2	S	•					Two-man catamaran.
Mystere	16.6	7.5	160	GRP	2	S	•					One-design catamaran with trapeze.
Nacra 18	17.0	10.0	192	GRP	1	U	•					Fast single-hander.
Nacra 5.2	17.1	7.9	219	GRP	2	S	•					Similar in concept to the Nacra 18, the 5.2 is a two-man boat.
Prindle 15	15.0	8.0	142	GRP	1	U	•		•			Racing single-hander that doubles as a beach boat.
Prindle 16	16.0	8.0	189	GRP	2	S	•		•			Two-man racing boat.
Prindle 18	18.0	8.0	217	GRP	2	S	•					Fast two-man catamaran.
Stampede	19.6	8.0	247	GRP	2	S	•					Twin wire racing catamaran.
Shearwater	16.6	7.6	360	GRP/Wood	2	S	•	•				Racing catamaran with spinnaker.
Spark	15.0	7.0	114	GRP	1	U	•		•			Una-rigged single-hander without boom.
Supercat	20.0	12.0	274	GRP	2	S	•					Fast, two-man racing cat.
Supercat 15	15.3	8.0	159	GRP	1	U	•					Racing single-hander.
Swift	14.6	5.1	130	GRP/Wood	2	S	•					Relatively old two-man racing catamaran.
Thundercat	18.0	8.0	240	GRP	2	S	•					Racing catamaran with two wires and Mylar sails.
Tornado	20.0	10.0	234	GRP	2	S	•	•		•	•	Olympic two-man catamaran.
Tri-Fli	14.0	8.0	105	GRP	1/2	U			•	•		Trimaran with outriggers. Sailboard style rig.
Unicorn	18.0	7.5	150	GRP	1	U	•	•				Una-rigged single-hander.

U = una rig
S = sloop rig

Trim and technique

Ian Fraser, twice world champion in the Tornado, once said, 'If you take your boat speed to be 100%, then your ability accounts for 80%, the set of the sails 17% to 18% and modifications designed to make the boat faster 2% to 3%. So if you are trailing behind, the fault lies first with yourself!'

We recommend displaying this wise statement in a visible place on the boat...

Trim begins with rigging up

Anyone who simply 'raises the rig on the cat' need not wonder why he never becomes world champion. If the mast leans like the famous tower of Pisa, the boat will simply not perform. Carefully check the length of the shrouds; they often differ by more than 'mere' millimetres! Bear in mind also that the shrouds, forestay and diamond stays of a new rig will stretch by up to 15 mm (0.5 in) when you sail in strong winds for the first time. Only then can you regard the lengths as final, provided they are not laid down by the boatbuilder. The degree of stretch varies according to the diameter of the wire!

As a rule, the mast should also be vertical fore and aft, that is to say perpendicular to the waterline. However, in many classes it has a pronounced rake aft. This trend began with the Hobies, was continued in the Dart and is now even found among the Tornados, where the American world champion Randy Smyth was a pioneer in this direction. In general, aft rake (diagram right) lowers the centre of effort of the sails slightly and produces a more open leech by closing up the mainsheet blocks, all benefits in strong winds. Numerous other trim factors also change, however.

If the mast of a catamaran with a boom is raked aft, the following happens:

A. The boat develops weather helm, the centre of effort of the sails moves aft

B. The leech of the jib opens

C. The foot of the jib tightens

The jib fairlead positions (F) may move forward

E. The distance between the mainsheet blocks closes (the blocks may become chock-a-block, so that the leech opens = H)

F. Jib fairlead positions move forward

G. The boom hangs lower across the trampoline

I. The load on the bridle increases

K. The load on the rudder increases

A boomless mainsail is affected in the same way as the jib:

D. Foot of the mainsail tightens

H. Leech of the mainsail becomes more open

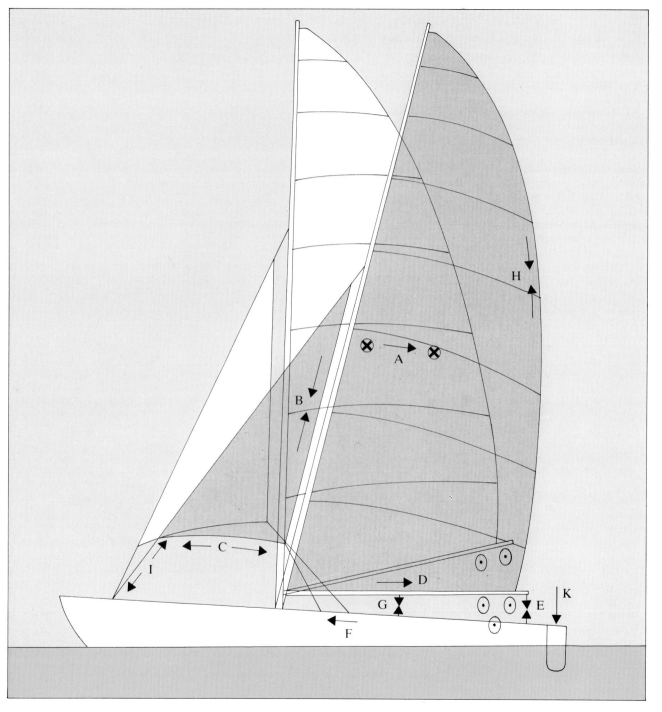

With a boomless rig, mast rotation is reduced, so that the mainsail must be trimmed flatter; the positions of the jib fairleads are no longer correct and must be recalculated.

It is inadvisable to make such drastic modifications without first discussing them with as many other owners of the same class of boat as possible. As a newcomer, you should first sail your cat as delivered by the builder or follow the example of the majority of sailors in the class. The photographs illustrate typical mast rake for Hobies. The general principle is to exercise great caution when making modifications to the rig, as they will affect the boat's behaviour.

A tip for the basic trim of your catamaran:

> When floating with both hulls immersed to the waterline, the boat should have slight lee helm.
> If it is sailed on one hull, it should have slight weather helm.

The first catamaran classes to have extreme mast rake aft were the Hobie 14 (left) and the Hobie 16. Trimming in this manner, which noticeably lifts the bows of the hulls, seems to have caught on for rough water sailing.

Mast bend: a blessing and a curse

It is not possible to prevent mast bend entirely, given the mast sections in common use today. Mast bend must therefore be controlled, allowing the mast to flex only as far as the sail requires.

Every mast has essentially two directions of bend with different degrees of stiffness; a mast section is stiffer fore and aft than athwartships. The overall bending characteristics of a mast are the product of these two components.

The fuller the cut of the sail, the more flexible the mast must be!

Hence, if you order a new mainsail you must tell the sailmaker the type and bending curve of the mast and the name of the manufacturer; if you don't, the new sail may be no more powerful than the old one.

In one-design classes you will not have to worry too much about these details, as the latitude is greatly restricted by the building rules and the sail specifications. In the case of racing catamarans, the class association's technical secretary or an experienced skipper will be best placed to advise you.

The diamonds also have a profound influence on the bending curve of a mast (photograph, below left). Their main function is to limit mast bend. In stiff rigs they are usually only a strut to prevent the masthead from bending to leeward and can therefore be made much lighter than for flexible rigs, where they must almost invariably cope with forces in several directions.

In general, it may be said that:

● Full-cut sails require more mast bend than flat ones.

● Light crews need a more flexible mast than their heavier counterparts.

● The stronger the wind, the flatter the sail must be trimmed.

Checking the rig

Before looking at the rest of the catamaran, you should check that:

● wires have no broken strands or sharp ends.

● all shackles are tightened with a shackle key.

● all split rings are securely taped.

● all split pins are bent over and bound with tape.

● all shroud bolts have the split ring inboard and taped.

● all telltales (cassette recording tape is ideal for this) are attached to the shrouds and the forestay bridle (see photographs, middle and right).

● the burgee has been mounted.

Don't feel ashamed if you have forgotten the burgee – you will not be the only one! To mount it at this stage, it is easier to lay the boat on its beam than to unstep the mast.

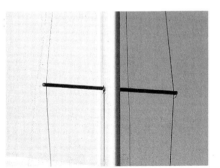

The single-spreader diamond rigging is not only common among sports catamarans, it is also the least complicated way of stiffening a rotating mast, unless it can be dispensed with entirely by using a suitable mast section, as in a large number of catamarans.

Telltales on shrouds and forestay bridle are essential for concentrated catamaran sailing. Strips of audio or video recording tape on the forestay have proved better than wool yarn or strips of spinnaker cloth (left). If the jib sets deep, the best place for the telltale is directly under the forestay bridle, as on the Stampede (right).

Good trim begins on land

The cat must track

If the cat does not point or perform as it should, take a close look at its track. To do this, the boat should be laid on trestles (on level ground, so that there is no twist in the boat) and its track and diagonals measured accurately (see the

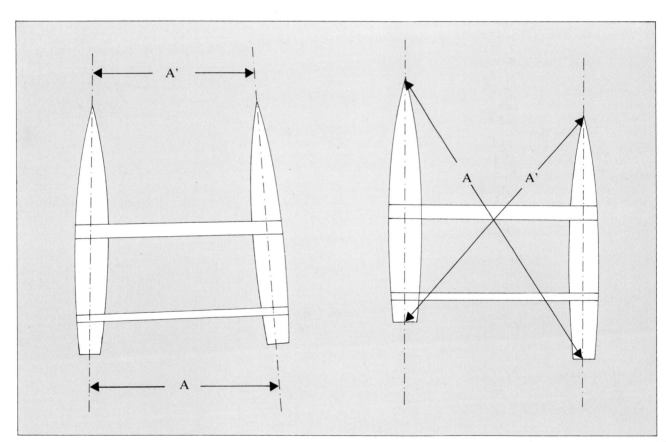

Measuring the track (left) and the diagonals. The maximum difference between A and A' should not be more than 1% of A.

Checking the rudder blades and centreboards for symmetry while the boat is on trestles: above = right, below = wrong.

diagram opposite). Even small discrepancies can have unwelcome effects, so that the tolerance should ideally be only 0.5% in the case of the track and 0.8% in the diagonal measurement. The maximum acceptable discrepancy is 1% in both cases.

While the boat is on trestles you can also check the centreboards and rudders. For this purpose, they must obviously be clean, in other words free of weed or road dirt, and should show no signs of damage. Dents and scratches should be filled, sanded and varnished or covered with gelcoat. Damage to the leading edge of a rudder or centreboard can reduce its hydrodynamic efficiency by up to 50%!

When you have done that, check that the play in the rudder trunks and centreboard cases is as small as possible, though not so small that the entire mechanism can be jammed by the slightest trace of sand, which the blades will quickly pick up.

The position of centreboards and rudders to one another and to the hull is just as important as perfect shape and surface finish.

Sight across the fully lowered boards to check that they match one another exactly (see the diagram below). In boats that have been in commission for

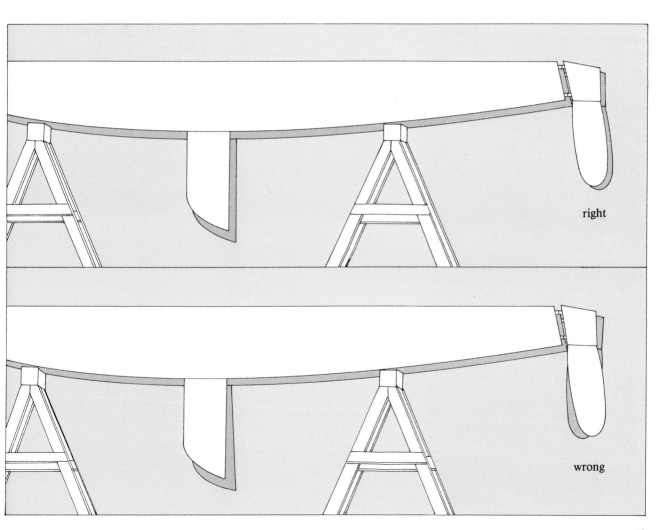

right

wrong

some time this is often no longer the case, for the boards are frequently let down with a jerk, which increasingly compresses the stops, often by different amounts on the two sides of the boat.

While you are checking the boards, mark on the deck or on the downhaul the various angles for raising the boards by a quarter, a half, and three-quarters; without these markings you will *never* raise the boards equally!

Now sight along the line of the keel from the bows and the stern (diagram below). This is the best way of seeing whether the boards are twisted, which has a very detrimental effect on boat speed. It is advisable to do the same with the rudder blades. Twist in rudders or boards should always be suspected if you detect sucking noises when the boat

is trimmed neutrally.

Like the centreboards, the rudder blades must be absolutely parallel (diagram right). To check this, raise the blades into the horizontal position, align them fore and aft and measure the distance between them at the mid point forward and at the extremity.

As with the centreboards, it is important that the rudder blades are identical (see diagram on page 49). If one blade is set further forward than the other, your cat will have greater lee or weather helm on one tack than the other. It is advisable to check the rudder blade stops regularly, for they also show wear as time goes on. This is one of the strengths of the daggerplate rudder, which is not subject to this type of wear.

If you think there is still something

wrong with the rudders, we recommend the following test. Trim the boat so that it will sail freely without rudder pressure. Disconnect the tiller bar and watch the rudders. A vibrating or oscillating rudder is not in good order. As a precaution, however, switch the port rudder to starboard and vice versa and repeat the test, for they can also be affected by damage to the hull.

If the boat develops lee or weather helm on different tacks despite perfectly trimmed sails and sailing on an even keel, check the centreboards and rudder blades for match, parallelity and twist!

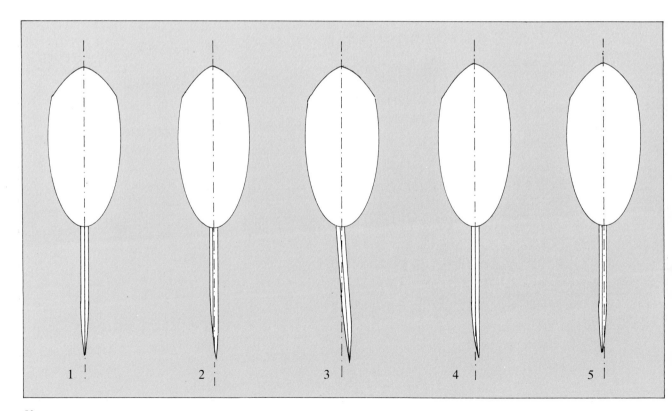

On the Ackermann effect...

...or: Rudolf Ackermann was wrong.

'Ackermann effect' is the term given to the intentional difference in rudder angles, which in the case of the catamaran is achieved by angling the tillers inwards. When the helm is put over, the rudder on the inside of the curve turns more sharply than the outside one, the argument being that the outside hull must be steered around a wider radius.

The idea was taken over from motor vehicle construction, where it is a necessary and sensible refinement because of the considerable friction between the tyres and the road surface. In the case of the catamaran, however, the friction between the water and the rudder blade is far less and you can safely spare yourself the effort; the gain is minimal.

max.
10 mm
(0.40 in)

Sighting along the line of the keel from the bow and from the stern shows whether the lowered centreboard is correctly positioned; 1 = correct, 2 = off centre, 3 = not perpendicular, 4 = twisted, 5 = not parallel with the keel line.

▲ *This is how to check that the rudder blades are parallel. Raise both blades, align one blade exactly with the centre line of the hull (a) and secure the tiller in this position. Now sight along centre line (b). The rudder blade of hull 'b' should look exactly the same as 'a', that is to say in alignment with the centre line of the hull. If the rudder blades are not in alignment, the discrepancy should be no more than 10 mm at the end of the blade.*

The better you set the battens, the better you will sail

The length and bending characteristics of the battens must suit the sail exactly. Your sailmaker generally cuts his sails to take a specific set of battens, so you should ask him which he recommends, unless the cut of the sail and the type of batten are laid down in the measurement rules.

When tying in the battens, ensure that the tension is equal on both ends of the lanyard (photographs below) and that the battens are properly seated in the batten pockets.

Battens have an unfortunate tendency to chafe through the cloth with alarming speed at the point where the sail presses against the shroud. A simple trick can help here (see photograph right, top).

As important as the choice of the batten set (the experts often take a considerable number of sets to a regatta) is the tension of the battens in the sail to suit the wind strength, the wave conditions and the weight of the crew.

It is therefore far from easy to find the most effective tension, for many factors cancel one another out. These general criteria will enable you to reach the best compromise for every crew in every situation.

> As a rule:
> – a lot of tension equates with deep sail camber
> – little tension gives a flat sail
> Hence tune the batten tension as follows:
>
> – light wind: a lot of tension
> – strong wind: little tension
> – light crew: less tension
> – heavy crew: more tension
> – little wave action: little tension
> – heavy waves: a lot of tension

As you have three criteria for batten tension – wind, crew weight and state of the water – always base your decision on the two dominant factors (see box).

Never tie in your battens 'this way because it's the way Joe does it'!

The best way to obtain an even sail shape is to lay the catamaran on its beam, haul the sheet tight and then tie in the battens (photograph right, bottom). By sighting from the masthead you can see precisely whether the shape is even throughout the sail.

Wood used to be a very popular materials for sail battens, but nowadays it is rarely used. Glass fibre is considerably more expensive, but good glass fibre battens last much longer, keep their shape better and even survive the occasional accidental gybe.

Solid battens and those made of GRP sandwich, mostly with foam cores, are both common. Sandwich battens are lighter, a distinct advantage when a set may have a total length of 15 metres (49.0 ft), for example. There is a drawback, however: they are more expensive than solid battens and many are also rather more susceptible to damage.

When tying in the sail battens, particular care must be taken to ensure even tension on both ends of the tie (left). The knot (middle) must be tight, but without overstraining the batten. Before finally tying off the knot (right), check the batten tension once again.

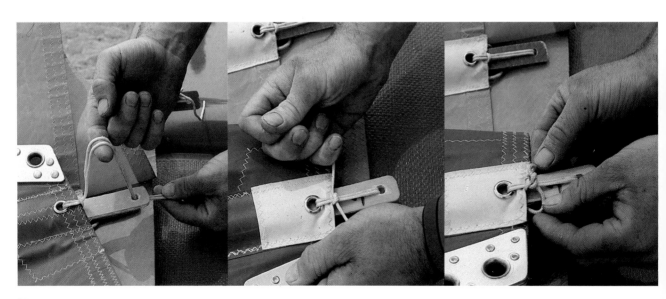

On a reach or a run, and especially in heavy seas, catamaran sails have the unpleasant tendency of chafing through at the points where the sail battens press the cloth against the shrouds. Wrapping the batten with soft foam (photograph) and reinforcing the sail at the points of contact cannot completely prevent chafe, but it will take about 15 times longer for the cloth to wear through. A good material for this is neoprene tape such as surfers us on their wishbone booms.

The easiest way of achieving an even sail shape is to tie in the battens after laying the cat on its beam and hauling in the sheet.

Hoist the sails

Catamaran sails must withstand much greater loads than the sails of conventional yachts, so that particular attention should be paid to workmanship and materials. It is strongly recommended that a new sail is ordered only from a sailmaker with proven experience in making catamaran sails. Ask around the class before ordering. In view of the high forces that develop, the cloth weight should not be less than 4 oz (US) (180g/m²).

The headboard, clew, tack and any reefing cringles must be particularly strong; you should not accept less than a sixfold reinforcement. The photograph shows reinforcement at the clew.

● The mast, sail and battens form a single unit and must therefore be precisely matched. The extent to which the shape of the sail can be altered by means of mast bend and batten tension is limited. The effect that changes in one of these components has on the other must be weighed up in advance.

● Large radius halliard sheaves make sail setting much easier. If the sail does 'jam', push the next panel into the luff groove by hand, but first check that the halliard lock is the right way round, otherwise you will have to start all over again.

● People sometimes forget to check whether the halliard lock has actually engaged, particularly when the mainsail can be raised only by main force. Watch out for that too!

Airflow – a smooth matter

For the catamaran, which is a high speed craft, streamlined airflow over the whole of the sail is of prime importance. Good sailors have a feel for it, but there are also aids that help show it. One is the wind direction indicator (mounted either at the masthead or under the forestay bridle), another is a series of telltales (photographs right). They are a very effective and above all a very cheap aid that has now caught on and proved its worth in monohulls as well as catamarans.

Many materials are used, depending more or less on personal preference: spinnaker cloth, magnetic tape and artificial yarn are all equally good.

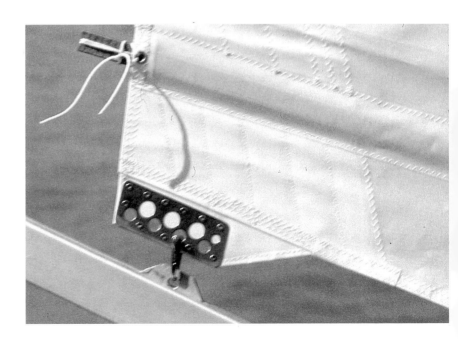

If the mainsail is loose-footed, tremendous loads are placed on the clew. The cloth must be reinforced at this point if it is not to tear out very quickly. The same applies to the area around the headboard.

A sail generates the greatest lift when the airflow is streamlined over both the windward and leeward sides of the sail. This can be monitored easily by fixing short telltales to both sides of the sail. Here all the threads are horizontal, so that the mainsail is setting perfectly. This principle applies to any windward course, whether beating (left) or reaching (right). (Windward telltales blue).

Wool yarn, on the other hand, is unsuitable, because it is not light enough when wet.

The telltales should be attached to both the jib *and* the mainsail. On the jib they should be fixed about 30 cm (12 in) behind the luff. Two or at the most three on each side of the sail are sufficient; too many only lead to confusion. The mainsail can have one telltale more per side. They should be attached about 30 cm (12 in) forward of the deepest point in the curve, including the mast. As a general principle, the sail should be sheeted and trimmed so that the telltales always lie horizontal on both sides of the sail.

If the telltale on the leeward side begins to flutter or even stands vertically, the mainsail is sheeted in too hard; if the one on the windward side flutters or lifts, the sail is too open and must be sheeted harder. The photographs illustrate the warning function of the telltales.

All the telltales must lie equally flat – on the windward and leeward sides, in the upper part of the sail and above the foot. If this cannot be achieved, go by the leeward telltales and check the trim of the entire rig when you return to land.

The mainsail of this Prindle 16 shows perfect airflow on the leeward side of the sail, although the traveller should be moved further to leeward. The jib is sheeted too hard, so that all the leeward telltales are fluttering; it is clearly beginning to backwind the mainsail.

In the case of the jib, if the upper telltales on the windward side flutter earlier than those in the lower part of the sail the fairlead must be moved forward; if it is the lower ones that break away first, the fairlead must be shifted further aft.

The same applies to the main, except that here nothing can be done about the sheeting position; fine-tuning is achieved by adjusting the luff, the traveller and above all the sheet.

Leech telltales, which are attached between the battens (photograph, page 58), have not yet caught on. Three are sufficient for the mainsail. When the sail is properly trimmed, these strips of material stream horizontally astern; if they flutter or blow forwards, they indicate that the airstream has separated on that side of the sail.

Obviously, telltales are useful only when there is airflow across the sail; on downwind courses they are no help at all.

● Never concentrate so hard on trimming aids that you take your eye off the situation or other competitors in a race!

● On land, practice adjusting the sails in accordance with the trimming aids by manoeuvring the cat into various courses on the trolley; when you are on the water you must be able to make the correct adjustment quickly and without thinking.

The windward telltales on the mainsail and jib of this Hobie 16 show that the airflow over this side of the sails has broken down. The helmsman should adjust the sheet and traveller settings as quickly as possible or change course.

All the windward telltales are lying flat, while those to leeward are turbulent. The sail is sheeted in too hard and should be eased. The airflow on the leeward side provides two-thirds of the sail's total drive, while that on the windward side generates only one-third. In case of doubt, the leeward telltales are therefore more important. (Windward telltales blue).

Because of twist, the telltales in the upper part of the sail are streamlined on both sides, but in the lower region only to windward. To make them lie flat throughout the sail, the traveller should be eased and then, if this is not enough, the mainsheet as well. (Windward telltales blue).

The three leech telltales can be seen on this Hobie 16. The two lower ones are streaming out cleanly, but there is turbulence around the top one; the leeward telltale in the sail also indicates this. All the other telltales are perfectly streamlined.

Trim, but don't overtrim

As fas as general sail trim is concerned, note that in most cases excessive muscle is a bad thing. If you use force, all that will happen will be that your sails will wear out faster than you or your wallet may like. In contrast to the foot and leech, the luff cannot or may not be adjusted underway on many cats. The ideal setting for the conditions must therefore be chosen on land.

Initially, the luff of the jib should be set up just hard enough to eliminate wrinkles. Mark this setting 'minimum'. This is also the correct setting for light winds, since the sail will then have a fuller camber.

As the wind increases, the luff of the jib needs to be tensioned harder to flatten the sail. Mark as the upper limit the point at which the tack of the jib will still go over cleanly and without backing when going about. If the tack remains wholly or partly on the wrong side it can cause the airflow over the entire lower part of the jib to break away (photograph above right).

Incidentally, before determining the minimum and maximum tension and the sheeting positions for a new jib you should allow it to stretch in moderate winds at the most; if you do so in strong winds, the sail may be completely distorted after only a few hours' sailing.

On most catamarans, the sheeting positions cannot be adjusted fore and aft. Nevertheless, check the position by hauling the sheet tight and twisting the leech and foot of the sail to ascertain whether the tension on each is equal (photographs below). You may be able to compensate for differences in tension by fitting an extra cringle in the tack or setting the jib higher or lower. If that is not enough, you should have a serious talk with your sailmaker.

On the other hand, many catamarans make provision for the jib sheeting position to be adjusted athwartships. The maxim here is: if in doubt, it is better to leave the sheeting position too far outboard than to move it too far inboard. Signs that the jib is backing the mainsail indicate that the jib fairlead is too far inboard.

Note that a fully-battened mainsail normally does not show that it is being backwinded until the dirty wind from the jib is putting considerable pressure

The jib tack attachment on this Tornado is excellent: there is a swivel between the luff tensioner and the tack so that even in light winds the jib will turn without twisting, which would cause the airflow to separate across the lower part of the sail. The tack is also held to the forestay by a second shackle so that the load on the sheet does not pull it aft, which would also distort the sail.

If the jib sheeting position is correct, the tension should be the same on the foot and the leech. The easiest way of checking this is by twisting the foot and leech between finger and thumb. If the foot is tighter than the leech, the jib sheeting position must be moved forward; if the leech is tighter, it must be shifted aft.

This procession of Prindles really makes you want to go catamaran sailing – come aboard!

on the leeward side of the sail. The jib must therefore be sheeted much further outboard than is indicated merely by the disappearance of the bulge in the mainsail.

The same principles apply to the mainsail. Mark as 'minimum' the luff setting that is sufficient to eliminate diagonal creases in the sail. There is hardly a maximum tension for the mainsail luff, except that imposed by your own strength and the workmanship of the sail. Here too, excessive loads are a bad thing if the sail has not yet been stretched; after that, however, too much tension on the luff is less damaging than too little. It takes less effort to tension the mainsail luff if you first haul the mainsheet taut.

● Jib: light luff tension gives a baggy sail for light winds; strong luff tension gives a flat sail for strong winds.

● Mainsail: light luff tension produces a flat sail for strong winds; strong luff tension gives a deep sail camber for light winds.

The diamonds

It is remarkable that there are still catamaran sailors who cannot tune the diamond rigging. In reality, it is quite simple:

● Slacker diamonds = more mast bend = less fullness in mainsail = setting for stronger winds.
● Tighter diamonds = less mast bend = more belly in the mainsail = setting for lighter winds.

The photograph shows how the tension of the diamonds can be tested.

Warning: as mast bend increases, so the support provided by the spreaders diminishes and there is the danger of buckling. Hence, the diamonds should never be too slack!

If the diamonds cannot be adjusted underway, they should be set permanently for strong winds as a precaution.

Enough of terra firma – let us get afloat!

As mast bend has a crucial influence on the set of the mainsail, the correct tension in the diamond rigging is very important. Above all, one must ensure that the loads are the same on both sides of the mast, otherwise it will bend to differing degrees in different directions and the catamaran will sail better on one tack than the other. A simple method of testing the tension of the diamonds is to press the wires against the mast with both thumbs; it is then easy to feel which side is under greater tension. The mast must be absolutely upright when you do this!

Catamaran sailing techniques

Ghosting is fun too!

Ghosting – fun? You probably think we are pulling your leg – but we're not.

Our first tip: make yourself comfortable and stretch out as flat as possible on your catamaran (see the photograph). The reason for this lies in the great concentration needed when sailing catamarans in light airs. You can concentrate only if you are sitting or lying in a relaxed and comfortable position, preferably lying while beating to windward because of wind resistance.

Here two Hobie 16 sailors demonstrate exemplary weight distribution on a beat in light airs. Shifting their body-weight forward raises the stern, so that the water can flow away better. At the same time the boat acquires slight weather helm, which greatly helps the helmsman to steer an optimum windward course in light airs.

The stern lifts out of the water, the transoms cannot cause drag, the waterline is shortened and the boat takes on slight weather helm. From his position the crew can better observe the telltales on the leeward side of the jib and the helmsman has a better feel for the boat than if the trim were completely neutral. At the same time, both of them have a good allround view, can spot wind shifts early and, if racing, can keep a close eye on the competition.

The angle of incidence of the mast depends largely on its section, the cut of the sail and the batten tension; as a rule, an angle of between 30° and 40° is appropriate for windward courses in light airs. Flexible masts must be angled more sharply than stiff ones.

The diamonds are set up hard; the mainsail luff must also be hauled as taut as possible to put draught into the sail. The jib luff, on the other hand, should be just taut enough to eliminate wrinkles. If the jib sheeting position is adjustable, move it slightly forward to increase the camber of the lower part of the foresail.

Both sails must be kept open; the airflow must be able to separate freely at the leech. Leech telltales are a great help in this situation.

In winds of force 2 or less the sheets should be handled very sensitively. Cleat them once you have found the correct setting and make any necessary corrections by adjusting your course; this will be more beneficial than trimming the sails every few minutes. In ghosting conditions the mainsheet traveller should be about a hand's breadth to leeward.

The centreboards and rudders should be fully lowered – in no event raise one of the rudder blades (photograph, page 65). If the wind does suddenly pick up, you will not be able to lower the blade in time. In any case, the rudder does more good than harm by smoothing the

Two requirements determine weight distribution on windward courses in light airs: first, body-weight must be shifted as far forward as possible and secondly windage should be as small as possible – the wind is blowing against you and trying to slow your progress. This single-hander is doing it right. The transoms of his boat are lifting free of the water and his half-lying position causes little wind resistance. To reduce it still further he would have to lie even flatter. However, he must inevitably sit up from time to time so that he can monitor wind shifts and other competitors more closely.

You should pay constant attention to the wind direction indicator, the telltales and, almost the most important of all, stillness aboard; jerky movements are to be avoided. Listen for noises too; gurgling or bubbling indicates that all is not as it should be.

Beating

To achieve ideal weight distribution, the crew should lie on the foredeck to leeward and the helmsman should sit directly aft of the main crossbeam to windward. This offers many advantages:

separation of the water flow at the stern; the hydrodynamic resistance of a single rudder blade is insignificant.

Reaching

Weight distribution can remain the same as on the beat; if necessary, the crew moves over onto the windward hull.

Leave the diamond setting as it was on the beat. However, the mast must be rotated as far as it is willing to go. It is even more important than on the beat to keep the leech of both sails completely open; the foot of the sails must have maximum camber.

Whereas on the beat it is correct to sail as close as possible to the wind and to react to any wind shifts by making course corrections, when reaching it is important to sail the shortest distance possible; in a race, for example, this will be a straight line from the windward mark to the reaching mark. Hence on this point of sailing the sheets are not cleated – the sail is trimmed to suit the course. Continual work on the sheets and attentive observation of the telltales bring the greatest dividends on this point of sailing.

The rudders should be left fully lowered, but the centreboards may be set according to the trim of the boat; they may be raised by as much as half if

Raising one rudder blade in light airs is a bad habit that is widespread but banned in many classes. If the boat is caught by a sudden gust from the wrong direction it may no longer be manoeuvrable. In any case, this cannot make the catamaran any faster, as the water resistance is insignificant at such slow speeds.

the boat will tolerate it. Trim should be as neutral as possible.

Running

Like any race, catamaran races are won on the finishing line, but the basis for victory or defeat is more likely to be laid on the downwind leg than in monohull races.

Catamarans differ from monohulls in that they can have laminar airflow across the sails downwind as well as to windward owing to their high potential speed. The much higher resultant drive enables them to sail to leeward much faster than conventional boats.

The secret lies in 'tacking downwind'. Every catamaran with a design, weight and rig that allow laminar airflow across the sails on courses of more that about 130° to the wind will make faster progress to leeward by tacking down-wind than if it were to sail the direct course.

The downwind leg is anything but easy in light airs. The first imperative is to sit still. Weight should be shifted as far forward as possible and the centreboards may be raised three-quarters or entirely, depending on the angle to the wind. As there is no longer airflow over the sails on this point of sailing, it is a question of catching every breath of wind as well as possible. The sailors in the A class catamaran (top) and Tornado (bottom) have even drawn up their legs to bring their weight well forward. A comfortable sitting position is particularly important downwind, because every movement causes the laminar hydrodynamic flow along the hulls to separate. As the telltales are useless on this point of sailing (they are clearly visible on the jib of the Tornado), the helmsman must rely on other signs. There are some who smoke downwind in light airs: cigarette smoke is a good wind direction indicator!

Here are a few typical classes and the wind strengths in which it pays to tack downwind:

Tornado   always (jib)
Hydra   always (jib)
Dart   from about force 2 (jib)
Hobie 18   from about force 2 (jib)
A Class cats from about force 2 (no jib)
Shearwater from about force 3 (jib)
Hobie 16   from about force 3 (jib)
Prindle 16 from about force 3 (jib)
Hobie 14   from about force 4 (no jib)
Topcat   from about force 4 (no jib)
Spark   from about force 4 (no jib)

We are dealing here with sailing in light airs, so the description of downwind tacking has been saved for the point where it is relevant to all types of catamaran: the section 'Moderate winds: sailing at its best.'

The selective list above shows that the majority of cats are best advised to follow the direct course to leeward in winds of force 2 or less.

Crew weight must be moved as far forward as possible (photographs, left). The man on the jib can even sit right up on the lee bow and boom out the jib by hand. The helmsman sits or stands on the windward end of the main crossbeam. He too keeps hold of the sheet and, if necessary, pushes the boom forward by hand. The mainsail must be set as open as possible.

Really smart catamaran sailors even ensure that when sitting or standing, they turn broadside to the breath of wind that can still be felt downwind so that they catch as much as possible. Perhaps this tactic really brings benefits for those who believe in it.

More important on the downwind leg is to keep absolutely still. The catamaran is now on its worst point of sailing; turbulence around the sails and the underwater body of the hulls caused by every sudden movement will make itself felt in terms of lost speed.

The mainsheet traveller is moved to the leeward end of the track and the centreboards are raised, but both rudder blades remain lowered even on this point of sailing.

Manoeuvring in light airs

Manoeuvring in light airs calls for sensitivity, above all else. 'Make haste slowly' is the first commandment, for when all is said and done frantic movement when tacking or gybing does not make the manoeuvre any faster. Smooth tiller control, gentle sheet handling and slow, co-ordinated movements produce the fastest progress for boat and crew. Always bear in mind that putting the rudder over too far costs you about a metre; if that happens ten times in the course of a race, your rival will be two boat lengths ahead by the finish!

A tack should only be commenced from a course hard on the wind, otherwise the cat will be caught in irons during the manoeuvre. The helm is put over very slightly at first and then further as speed is lost. At the same time, helmsman and crew move as far aft as possible to enhance the turning tendency by lightening the bows.

Depending on the rudder profile, the flow along the blade will separate sooner or later if you change the angle of incidence. Particularly slow or fast

motion through the water accelerates this process, so you should always avoid putting the helm over too far; as a general guide, the limit should be between 12° and 30°, depending on boat speed. Beyond that the flow will separate even with a 'kindly' profile, so that the rudder will have little more than a braking effect. You can do without that, particularly in light airs.

The sheets are eased as soon as the boat goes through the wind and they are not hardened in again until the cat has borne well away onto the new tack. First the jib is sheeted in and then the mainsail, which is given a quick jerk on the boom to make the battens spring to leeward (photographs on the following pages).

If the cat misses stays despite all precautions, do not panic and do not thrash frantically with the rudder! Reverse the helm, let the sails go completely and wait until the boat has developed enough sternway to turn onto the new tack.

If the wind is so light that this would take too long, this little ploy will help: raise both rudder blades halfway, pull the tiller back towards you slowly and then push it away smartly (see photograph page 70). This should usually be enough to bring the catamaran onto the new tack. 'Waggling' the tiller to and fro with the rudder blades down is not very effective. Now drop the rudder blades and trim the sails for the new course.

Little needs to be said about gybing in light winds. The boom is simply put across and the battens are sprung over. This will produce a slight increase in speed; when racing, however, do not be tempted to make one gybe after another for the entire downwind leg; the other competitors won't like it...

Tacking a one-man catamaran, demonstrated by a Topcat in light winds:

Sensitive tiller action causes the boat to luff in a wide curve

As the boat passes through the eye of the wind the mainsheet is uncleated and eased

The traveller can then easily be pushed into the new leeward position

The helmsman turns to face aft...

The helmsman bears away slightly below the new course to ensure that the catamaran will pick up speed when the mainsail is sheeted in

... and swings the tiller extension over to the new side without upsetting the boat's head by making false rudder movements

And away on the new tack!

If the catamaran misses stays, it can be brought round onto the new course by raising the rudder blades halfway and pushing the tiller smartly. Similarly, in a calm, the boat can be moved forward by repeated 'waggling' of the tiller. Initially, the movements must be large, but as the boat picks up speed they can be shorter. Note that this trick is not permitted while racing.

Moderate winds: sailing at its best

Creaming along in a fast cat in winds of force 3 or 4, shooting across the water at top speed – that is the catamaran sailor's dream. You never tire or become bored. It is pure speed with practically no danger of capsizing or damaging equipment. You don't even mind losing a race when the conditions are so marvellous!

Moderate winds are also ideal for trimming the boat, practising manoeuvres (which you cannot do often enough) and trying out tactical ideas. It provides equally good conditions for testing new wardrobes of sails and for carrying out capsize drill, although for safety's sake you should be accompanied by a second boat when you do this.

In moderate winds you will use a new piece of equipment to trim the boat: the trapeze.

The trapeze

Before examining the various points of sailing, a few general remarks about this aid to boat trim. The most important item is a good quality, well-fitting trapeze belt (see photographs), or better still a trapeze harness. It must be snug without being tight. Padding in the seat and across the back are not a luxury but give the wearer greater comfort and thus improve his concentration. A trapeze harness should not sink if it is washed overboard when not being worn, but is should not have so much buoyancy that it can turn the wearer face-down in the water if he should fall overboard. It must be adjustable around the legs, in the length of the back and around the waist and once the buckles have been adjusted they should hold securely. The higher the back support, the better; the wider the harness, the more comfortable it will be.

If you trapeze on a catamaran, you should not hang out as flat as on monohulls, for at normal catamaran sailing

A good trapeze harness should look like this. The most important point is firm seat support, which can only be achieved if the harness is sufficiently adjustable. The hook must be set low (left) and the back should reach as high as possible over the shoulders (right). Anyone who has landed heavily on the rubbing strake when swinging back aboard will no longer regard firm padding as an unsportsman-like luxury.

On inland waters the trapeze should allow you to hang at about deck level at full stretch; on open water 15cm to 20cm (6in to 8in) higher is better. These two G-Cat sailors are a little too low and they should stand with their feet further apart.

The stance demonstrated by this Wing sailor is excellent. Only by placing his feet well apart does the single-hander have the necessary security when trapezing.

speeds the pounding of the waves can not only give the man on the trapeze a heavy beating but may also fling him aft and noticeably reduce the boat's speed. It also makes it more difficult to come back aboard.

As a rule, the crew should already let the trapeze bear his weight when he is sitting out on the gunwale.

Catamarans with provision for a trapeze must also be equipped so that it can be used safely as well as effectively. Foot loops on the edge of the deck are absolutely essential (photograph, page 74). They must be fitted in such a way that they remain open so that the man on the trapeze can slip his feet into them without fumbling. They must also be large enough to ensure that his feet cannot be trapped in them in an emergency.

Another aid, especially for reaching and running, is the restraining line (photograph, page 76). Its length is adjusted to suit the man on the trapeze. Here too, it is important to ensure that it can be attached and unattached quickly with one hand, the other being

In medium winds the crew hooks on the trapeze and sits far enough out for it to bear his weight and make sitting out less tiring. If the hull suddenly begins to lift in a gust he can immediately swing outboard without losing time fumbling with the trapeze gear.

Foot loops on the gunwale should be so fitted that they do not lie flat on the hull but stand well away - it it then quicker to slip your feet into them. They must also be fixed very securely, because they are often wrongly used when carrying the catamaran.

The crew on this Tornado is preparing to go into the trapeze, but he has not yet hooked on. It would be much better - and safer - if he hung further outboard after hooking on. Time and again, slack trapeze gear comes unhooked without the wearer noticing. He then launches himself outboard - and finds himself swimming!

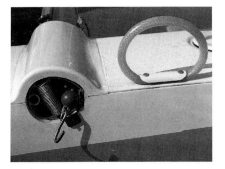

This restraining line on a Stampede is simply a small S-shaped hook held in the aft crossbeam by means of shockcord when not in use (right). If the trapezing crew is standing far enough aft on a reach, he pulls the hook out of the crossbeam and hooks it onto the trapeze ring. If he also has his feet in foot loops of adequate size, he will remain where he belongs on this course, namely aft, even after a sudden nosedive.

needed for the sheet. The man on the trapeze must also have a firm footing, irrespective of these items of equipment. This is generally achieved by applying anti-slip tape, which is available from a number of manufacturers.

Any sailor who uses the trapeze must always wear shoes!

Do not spring to the trapeze immediately a gust comes. If it is only shortlived it is better to ease the sheets a little, and thus allow the boat to run on smoothly, than to be constantly jumping in and out of the boat.

Beating

In moderate winds the helmsman and crew will aim to trim the boat so that the lee bow has just enough freeboard to cope with the waves; they will therefore sit just aft of the main crossbeam (photograph right, top).

They should sit very close to one another (photograph right, bottom) to reduce wind resistance as much as possible, and should have their feet hooked under the toestraps, which should preferably be padded.

It is the job of the helmsman to keep the catamaran 'in suspension', whether the crew is trapezing or not. Assuming the wind is steady, the most the man on the trapeze should do to help is to flex his knees a little more or a little less. If the wind is not always strong enough to trapeze, it is more sensible if both sit out on the gunwale and cope with any occasional gusts by easing the sheets if luffing is not sufficient.

Never let the windward hull fly too

high, for you will count the cost in terms of lost speed (photographs, page 78 left). It is better to trim the boat so that the hull occasionally brushes the waves, for this will barely check your way. As there is a slight lag before the airflow across the sail becomes effective, it is particularly important to stay alert. Hence you should luff slightly even as the cat begins to lift and bear away gently when you feel the windward hull begin to sink back. The sooner you react, the more precisely you will be able to keep the catamaran in ideal trim athwartships. If the fore and aft trim needs to be adjusted, it is sufficient for one man to change position.

The mast is rotated slightly less than in light winds; depending on the rig, the angle to the centreline will be somewhere between 30° and 45° (diagram, page 79). The diamonds are not quite as taut as in light winds, but still not slack.

The luff of the mainsail should also be slacker than in light winds, but the jib luff should be set up harder. The mainsail clew outhaul (photographs, page 78 right) is hauled almost to the aft stop, leaving only about 10% camber in the sail. The leech is trimmed almost closed.

The mainsheet is hauled tight and cleated, but held in the hand because of possible gusts; on most boats the traveller is set about 20 cm – 25 cm (8 in – 10 in) leeward. The jib sheet is also hauled in; the crew should pay particular attention to the telltales on the leeward side of the mainsail so that he can quickly recognise the danger of backwinding the main.

As in light airs, adjustments on the beat should generally be made first by altering course, using small rudder angles; brisk movements merely serve to slow the cat down. The centreboards and rudder blades must of course be fully lowered.

In light to medium winds the helmsman and crew should shift their weight as far forward as possible, lifting the stern and allowing the water to separate more smoothly at the transom as the keel rocker is eased. This A Class cat demonstrates exemplary weight distribution.

Crew and helmsman on this Tornado are sitting close together on either side of the shroud. It can be seen clearly that trimming the weight so far forward frees the transoms. Although the windward hull is on the point of lifting out of the water, the transom of the lee hull is still not immersed.

The view is undoubtedly better if you fly a hull as high as this, but the effect on speed will be very detrimental. Both the Hobie 18 (top) and the Tornado (bottom) are clearly one storey too high and cannot by this means convert the power of the sail into speed.

In a great many racing catamarans the clew outhaul runs inside the aluminium section of the boom. This can be seen clearly on the Wing catamaran illustrated: in the top photograph the foot has been hauled taut for the beat, while in the bottom photograph it is slack for reaching, thereby inducing greater sail camber. ▼

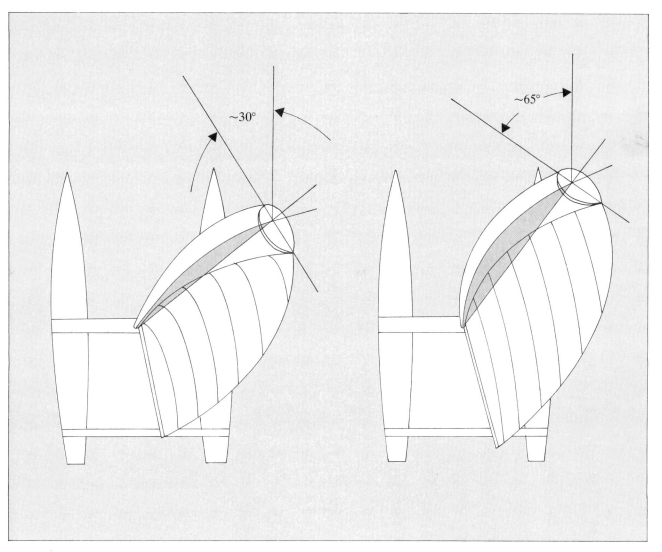

Effect of mast rotation on mast curvature and sail camber:
Left = slight mast rotation:
– marked bend to leeward
– slight bend forward
– deep sail camber

Right = prounounced mast rotation:
– slight bend to leeward
– prounounced bend forward
– flat sail

Reaching

When reaching, weight should be distributed so that the lee bow always has reserve freeboard of 10 cm (4 in), which should be enough to prevent the bow burying itself in 'normal' gusts. If you see a particularly strong gust coming, trim the boat noticeably by the stern *before* the gust strikes – it is easier to move forward than aft! As before, the

helmsman and crew should sit close together so that they cause little wind resistance. The trapeze is unlikely to be used in these conditions and the crew can have his feet under the toestraps, but as a precaution he should also be hooked onto the trapeze.

The mast must now be rotated as far as possible, while leaving diamond tension the same as on the beat. The luff of the jib is set slightly slacker than on the beat, but the mainsail luff remains under moderate tension as before. The foot is adjusted to produce moderate sail camber (20% – 25% can be taken as a guide) and the leech of the mainsail is given a slight twist.

By twist we mean that the angle of incidence varies over the height of the sail (see the photograph). This is really something that one prefers to avoid for aerodynamic reasons, but it does have one advantage: as the angle of incidence is not uniform, the separation of the airflow at *one* point does not mean that the entire sail becomes ineffectual or underpowered, for the angle of incidence of one part of the sail is now exactly right and that part is drawing fully. The more frequently the angle of incidence is temporarily altered by wave action, short-lived gusts, disturbed wind or tactical moves, the more important twist becomes.

Twist can be produced by easing the mainsheet but leaving the traveller cleated in the correct position. The greater the sheeting angle to the clew, the greater the twist.

The mainsheet is now held uncleated and the lifting of the windward hull is controlled via the sheet.

By twist we mean a pronounced falling away of the mainsail leech. The photograph shows clearly how the upper part of the sail is sagging to leeward while the lower part is sheeted hard in. This means that only the middle third of the sail is producing full drive. Even on this boat the traveller should be eased as quickly as possible to leeward. Slight twist in the leech of the sail is admissible only if the helmsman has to luff and bear away continuously to make best use of the waves; here it is excessive in any case.

Warning: the more the boat rises, the greater the tendency for the lee hull to bury itself (see the photographs on page 81)! Hence, keep the windward hull as low as possible above the water.

The jib sheet is also controlled by hand; both sails are trimmed as precisely as possible according to the telltales. Depending on the course, the traveller is half way or wholly to leeward, the boat remains exactly on course for the finish and the airflow across the sails is kept streamlined by working the sheets.

The rudder blades obviously remain in their lowest position and the centreboards are between half raised and fully lowered, depending on trim.

> General principle for twist: as much as is absolutely necessary, but as little as possible!

◀ *The helmsman of this Unicorn has borne away without moving his body-weight further aft; he is still in the same position as for the beat. As this classic nosedive shows, his boat has taken it very badly indeed and has buried the lee bow.*

◀ *The lee bow of this Tornado is already close to the limit; there is no buoyancy in hand for a gust. That may be acceptable in smooth water, but in a seaway it is certainly not to be recommended, as the tip of the bow should be at least two hand breadths above the surface of the water. A further disadvantage is that the rudder blades are lifted increasingly out of the water as the bows dip, so that the catamaran becomes more and more difficult to manoeuvre, particularly at high speed.*

Fly, Hobie, fly. This sailor will not reach optimum speed, but what could be finer than hovering between the water and the sky, the light and the air?

Running

In most types of catamaran, tacking downwind already begins to pay in winds of force 3 or 4. The exact point at which this means of approaching the finishing line to leeward becomes profitable depends mainly on the construction of the cat (see page 67) and the height of the waves.

The higher the waves, the sooner it pays to tack downwind, as the waves travelling to leeward provide additional power. Anything that helps the catamaran sail faster also favours downwind tacking.

It is not an easy decision for the helmsman, and it is primarily a matter of experience and feel. A true gain can be made only within the narrow confines of the ideal combination of two contradictory demands:

The first is the ground gained to leeward. In normal circumstances, the shorter the distance sailed to leeward, the greater the ground gained. Taken on its own, ground gained to leeward would therefore militate in favour of the direct course, as described in the chapter on the downwind leg in light airs.

The second component is the speed gain. Whereas the need to gain ground to leeward tempts the helmsman to bear away in order to sail a short course, the prospect of a gain in speed forces him to luff up, for only then will the cat readily accelerate.

The net result: those who sail too far off the wind have a shorter distance to cover but at a slower speed, while those who sail too close to the wind travel faster but have to sail considerably further (see diagram overleaf).

Finding the ideal track therefore requires a calculation of distance versus speed, which has to be solved by instinct on small catamarans rather than by the on-board computer, as on an Admiral's Cupper.

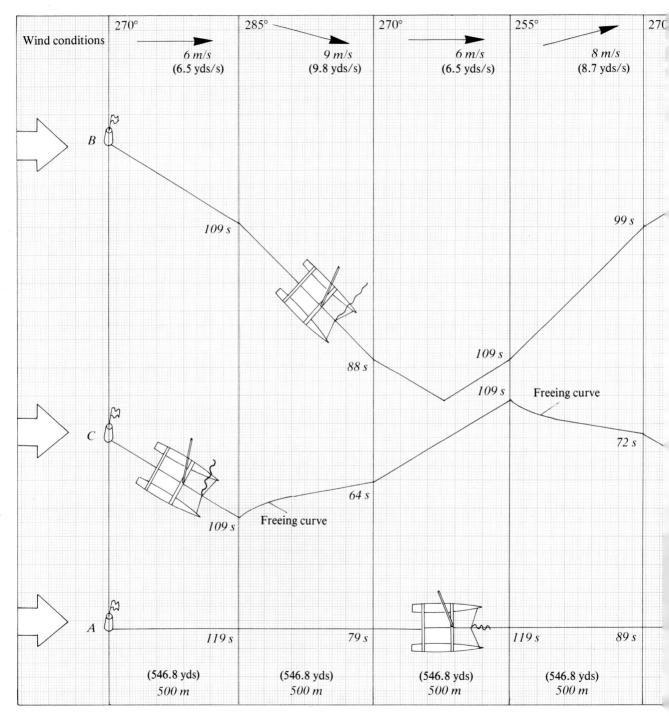

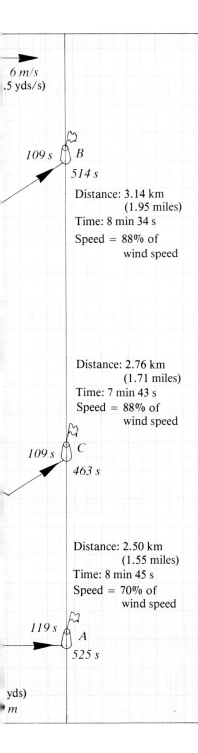

6 m/s
.5 yds/s)

109 s B
514 s

Distance: 3.14 km
(1.95 miles)
Time: 8 min 34 s
Speed = 88% of
wind speed

Distance: 2.76 km
(1.71 miles)
Time: 7 min 43 s
Speed = 88% of
wind speed

109 s C
463 s

Distance: 2.50 km
(1.55 miles)
Time: 8 min 45 s
Speed = 70% of
wind speed

119 s A
525 s

yds)
m

Tacking downwind:

A   *is being sailed by a beginner who has still
not heard of tacking downwind. He sails
the shortest distance dead before the wind
and takes 8 minutes 45 seconds, if we
assume his boat speed to be 70% of the
wind speed. Airflow across the sail is not
streamlined.*
B   *tacks doggedly leeward according to the
telltales and the airflow, without regard
for wind shifts. Despite the much longer
distance sailed, the boat reaches the buoy
at almost the same time as A.*
C   *is being sailed by a cunning fox who gybes
at each wind shift and sails a smooth
freeing curve when the wind strengthens.
He gains more than a minute over A and
B, worth almost 200 metres (656 feet) on
the following beat! In practice, careful
surfing before the waves will increase the
lead even further.*
*Conclusion: Downwind, the catamaran sails
at 70% of the wind speed; the optimum
tacking course to the leeward is about 30°.
The increase in speed as a result of tacking is
18% of the wind speed (16% would be
enough to make up for the greater distance
sailed).*

One of the most important requisites
for successful downwind tacking is an
ability to recognise whether the airflow
across the sails is still laminar on such a
course.

> The secret of tacking downwind lies
> in sensing changes in speed immedi-
> ately!

The real difficulty with tacking downwind is that one never sails in a straight
line, since to be successful the helmsman must steer two opposing curves
which are in turn dependent on two
factors: speed and angle to the wind.

Only by first sailing an 'acceleration
curve' (see page 89) does the catamaran
pick up sufficient speed to be able to
bear away and sail a 'freeing curve'
without significant loss of way.

As far as the question whether to tack
downwind or not is concerned, you can
begin by following the example of the
race leaders; if the majority choose to
tack downwind, you should follow suit,
even if you still have little experience of
this technique.

You will always be on your own when
it comes to deciding the angle to sail,
for on the downwind tack the field
usually scatters in all directions; from
your position to windward you will find
it almost impossible to say who is in the
lead and why, for each cat will be sailing its own individual acceleration or
freeing curve. Even if you are watching
closely, it is very difficult to ascertain
which curve a particular catamaran is
sailing at any particular time. In any
case, during a race you will not have the
time (or the composure) to observe
another boat for minutes on end.

Even before rounding the windward
buoy you should have spotted which
side of the course is favoured. This is
generally easy to see; as on a normal
beat, there is almost always a favoured

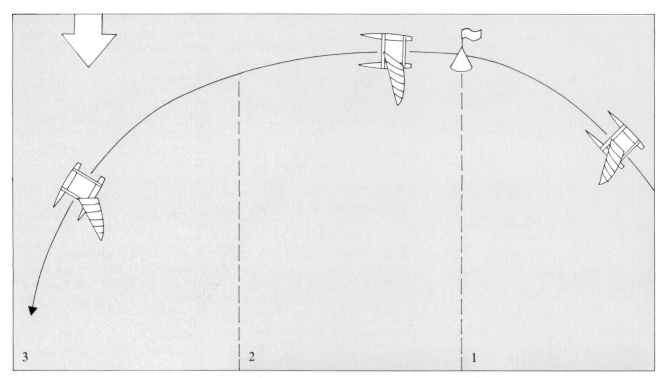

3   2   1

Bearing away at the windward mark:
1 Bear away gradually after the beat
2 Gain maximum speed with wind abeam
3 Bear away gently and use the speed to run
further off the wind.

The helmsman of this O.K. catamaran is
rounding the windward mark sensitively in a
wide arc, easing the sheet and the traveller as
the angle of the apparent wind changes. The
knack is to carry the higher speed as far as
possible on the windward beat.

side which will bring you closer to the buoy than if you had chosen the other.

The favoured side for the beat to windward is also the favoured side for tacking downwind. If you chose the wrong side for the conventional beat, remember to take the other side for the downwind tacking leg.

Having chosen the favoured side, bear away smoothly to gain speed (diagram left). Bearing away sharply immediately after rounding the buoy and sailing downwind brings no advantage; if instead you bear away slowly and use a little skill, the speed you will pick up on the resultant short reach can be maintained for some time.

From now onwards, rudder movements should be kept to the absolute minimum to prevent separation of the flow across the sails and rudder blades (see photographs).

If you put the helm up too abruptly when bearing away and at the same time forget to ease the mainsheet, the flow over the rudder blades will break away. Approaching from the windward leg, this Wing helmsman bears away slightly before the buoy and then alters course sharply at full speed right at the buoy. . .

. . . with the result that the rudder blades lose their steering effect and simply throw up an impressive fountain of water.

Bear away smoothly until the apparent wind is more or less abeam, as shown by the telltales on the forestay bridle, not the wind vane, for if you watch the latter you will lose your overall view of the leg, and you will get a stiff neck.

It is also important to observe the course angle to the leeward buoy. If it is more than 45° you are on the wrong side and should gybe. If it is less, you can continue on this gybe until it exceeds the 45° limit.

If the apparent wind moves abaft the beam you will notice a drop in speed. Luff boldly, but with the minimum rudder movement, until the cat again accelerates (1–3 in the diagram), then bear away again very, very slowly and try to maintain speed. This manoeuvre of bearing away as far as possible without losing speed is the very essence of a perfectly executed downwind tack.

The ideal downwind tack therefore consists in sailing the catamaran as far as possible in a freeing curve without the airflow across the sails breaking away (4–6 in the diagram).

If you have sailed too far off the wind and the cat slows down noticeably, the only remedy is to luff up rapidly. However, this should be regarded as an emergency measure; gradual course corrections should be the rule.

So how do you gain speed? That is not so difficult: luff up until the wind is slightly forward of the beam. The cat will now accelerate noticeably and the

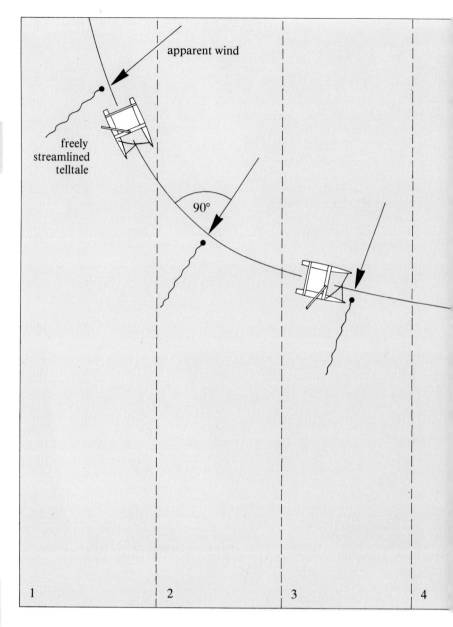

apparent wind will therefore move still further forward. Counteract this by bearing away in a smooth curve, carefully watching the telltales under the forestay bridle and in the sails. The further you bear away, the harder you must concentrate, and if the wind begins to move abaft the beam you must immediately try to maintain speed by luffing up. The ideal is to keep the apparent wind constantly more or less abeam.

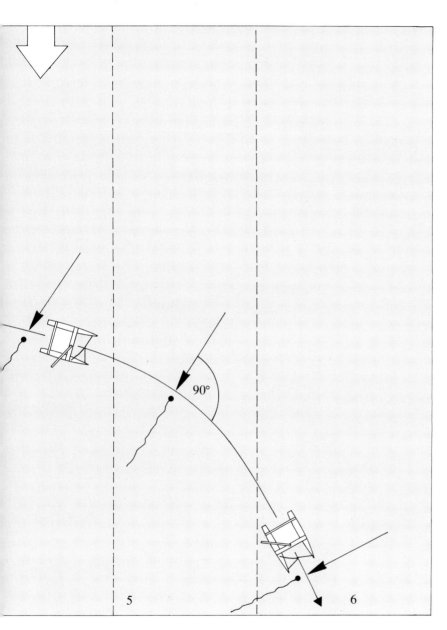

Acceleration curve:
1 – The boat slows down, sails too far off the wind, the airflow breaks away
  – Apparent wind comes from abaft the beam
  – Telltale creeps forward
2 – Boat luffs up and accelerates again, the airflow becomes laminar
  – Apparent wind moves forward of the beam
  – Telltale shifts abaft the beam
3 – Boat has regained full speed, the airflow is fully streamlined
  – Apparent wind from a few degrees forward of the beam
  – Telltale flies slightly abaft the beam

Freeing curve:
4 – Boat is sailing at full speed, the airflow is fully streamlined
  – Apparent wind comes from a few degrees abaft the beam
  – Telltale flies slightly abaft the beam
5 – Boat bears away smoothly, maintaining speed, airflow fully streamlined
  – Apparent wind remains slightly forward of the beam and abeam
  – Telltale remains between slightly abaft the beam and abeam
6 – Steer the boat as far as possible off the wind without losing speed or disturbing the laminar airflow
  – Apparent wind fluctuates between slightly forward of the beam and abeam
  – Telltale fluctuates between slightly abaft the beam and abeam

If the telltale again creeps forward, luff up immediately, sail an acceleration curve, and so forth.

from the telltales: the helmsman's bottom. If you train this part of your anatomy to sense changes in boat speed, it will often warn you sooner than the telltales.

Pay particular attention to gusts. The early recognition and exploitation of gusts can give you a substantial lead over the opposition in a matter of minutes, for every gust allows you to sail a little further off the wind.

The higher wind speed in the gust brings the apparent wind forward and allows you to bear away further and begin a new freeing curve.

There is yet another important 'instrument' for tacking downwind apart

Tacking downwind is a matter of feel. Even for those with a natural talent, perfection comes only as a result of much practice.

Traveller angle

As the wind strengthens, a further trimming device becomes increasingly important: the traveller.

Its main purpose is to change the sail's angle of incidence to the wind without inducing twist. The ideal solution is a traveller riding on a semi-circular track with the axis of the mast at its centre (photograph below). This is the normal arrangement on C Class catamarans, but it has not caught on in the A and B Classes, as it is more difficult to construct and is also susceptible to damage.

The basic rule is to set the traveller sufficiently far to leeward so that, with the mainsail sheeted in, rudder movements alone will keep the boat in equilibrium with the windward hull just lifting, for only an even sail profile set as perpendicular to the surface of the water as possible develops maximum lift.

It appears that not everybody has yet heard of the benefits of this trimming device, although there are few

Semi-circular traveller tracks allow the sail to be trimmed over a wide range of angles without twist. However, this requires a relatively large design effort that is normally undertaken only in out-and-out racing catamarans such as those in C Class. The example illustrated here on an O.K. is therefore rather an exception – or a pointer to the future?

Concentration is everything when the course becomes crowded. This Nacra crew only have eyes for the opposition.

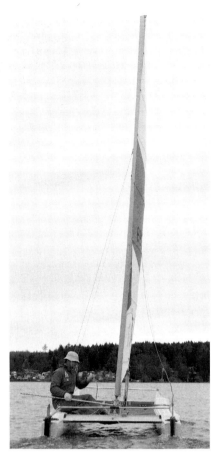

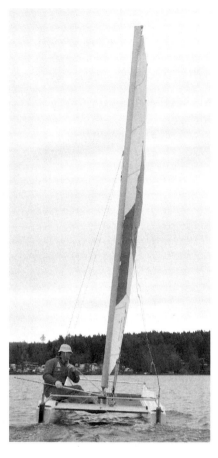

The wind must be able to separate freely from the leech of the sail and should on no account be treated roughly at this point, which is important for boat speed. Even the smallest alteration in sheeting produces major changes in the sail. In the left-hand picture the sail is sheeted too hard and is closing at the leech. In the centre photograph the sail trim is optimum, while in the right-hand picture the leech is too open, wasting power.

catamarans that do not now offer it as standard equipment. Hence our tip that will probably draw a laugh from experienced catamaran sailors: if your cat has a traveller, use it!

When you consider how important the traveller is for boat trim, it is a mystery why many newcomers cannot get the hang of it and therefore leave the car in one position. It is really as simple as pie:

- The broader the wind, the further outboard the traveller must go.
- If the boom is over the traveller track, the mainsail should be sheeted tight.
- If the windward hull lifts too far, the traveller should be moved further outboard.
- Conversely, if you feel that the sail is providing too little power, the traveller should first be brought closer to the centreline.
- The harder it blows, the further outboard the traveller must be set, even on the beat!

Manoeuvring in moderate winds

One might say it is all the helmsman's fault if a manoeuvre is bungled in moderate winds, and indeed every manoeuvre should be successful in these conditions. As in light winds, the tack should be begun only from a course hard on the wind (see photographs); then it can really only be spoilt by moving the rudder too quickly. Depending on the area, there may already be some chop in winds of force 4; if that is the case, tacking can be made easier by timing it so that the centreboards are on the crest of a wave while the turning moment is greatest.

4 The helmsman fishes the tiller extension out of the water and settles into his new seating position; the crew clips on the trapeze gear and swings outboard as the helmsman sheets in the mainsail.

3 The helmsman and crew shift to the new windward side. As soon as the sails come across, the jib is sheeted in and the mainsheet eased. The boat should turn through the wind beyond the new windward course. The battens are sprung across by giving a sharp tug on the boom or on the mainsheet tackle, as here.

2 The helmsman then grips the tiller bar and puts the helm down smoothly but increasingly, so that the boat turns through the wind in an arc.

1 Tacking a two-man catamaran, in this instance a Dart: the crew on the trapeze returns to the trampoline and uncleats the jib sheet; the helmsman does the same with the mainsheet and throws the tiller extension aft into the water. ▶

Gybing is also completely uneventful in these wind conditions (see photographs). However, if you feel shaky about it, even in winds of force 4 you can commence the gybe with a freeing curve as on the downwind tack. As soon as the boat speed drops noticeably, the skipper puts the helm over.

With his free hand he then grasps the mainsheet tackle and brings the sail onto the new leeward side. Some of the shock on the mainsail as it goes over should be taken by hand. The mainsail is not sheeted tighter immediately. Hauling in the mainsheet before gybing as on traditional yachts is not only unnecessary on a catamaran but also detrimental, as it wastes time and the gybe no longer takes place when the boat is travelling as fast as possible, when the apparent wind is automatically less.

Before gybing, check that the sheet and traveller are free so that they can go over without snagging.

7 . . . and moves forward to the main crossbeam for the downwind leg

6 Now the helmsman luffs up until the telltales are again lying quietly . . .

5 . . . and takes the mainsheet tackle in his other hand so that as the boat turns through the wind he can pull the mainsheet and the traveller onto the new side. The traveller must be prevented from slamming into the stops and the battens from hitting the shroud by taking the weight on the parts of the mainsheet tackle, particularly in strong winds; otherwise damage might ensue

1 Gybing a single-handed catamaran, demonstrated here in light winds aboard a Topcat. The helmsman shifts aft from his downwind position on the main crossbeam...

2 ...and begins to bear away in a smooth curve

4 ...grasps it to leeward (he could equally well throw it into the water aft, as when tacking, and steer with the tiller bar)...

3 Then he lays the tiller extension on the new side...

When it's blowing half a gale...

...catamaran sailing is still a lot of fun, indeed for many people the fun does not really begin until force 5 or 6.

But hold on! Sailing catamarans or dinghies in strong winds is a matter of practice, and no-one should begin to learn in winds of force 6. Boat control comes with training and familiarity with the boat. It is therefore advisable to tackle the next highest wind force only when you have firm mastery of the cat in lighter winds.

Mental attitude is important for sailing in strong winds, far more so than in light winds. A sailor who is rigid with fear or uncertainty is unlikely to be able to assess the situation correctly and will therefore make mistakes that will turn the outing into a fiasco.

Never set out in a strong wind just so that you will not be thought a coward!

Beating

In strong winds, crew weight must be distributed to suit the wave conditions as well as the wind. Closehauled, the boat should be trimmed as far forward as possible, but also as far aft as is necessary; if in doubt, it is better to have a little too much weight in the stern than in the bows. The leedeck must be kept free of solid water!

The helmsman will therefore sit about midway between the shroud plate and the aft crossbeam and the crew will trapeze just forward of him. If the waves are not too short, they should both lean aft before a wave arrives to ease the bows but then lean forward again to keep the stems in the water so that the cat cannot develop lee helm. The helmsman's feet must be held securely by the toestraps and the crew must have a firm footing on the gunwale. Roughened standing areas are a help, or better still foot loops that prevent the crew losing contact with the boat.

The man on the trapeze should keep his knees slightly bent so that he can absorb the cat's movements in the waves. Standing with his feet apart will also help give him a secure footing, but how far apart will depend on the ability of the helmsman.

It deserves to be emphasised that crews flying out of the trapeze are always the fault of the helmsman taking a wave wrongly, spotting a squall too late or making a course correction too abruptly.

According to the latest aerodynamic teaching on mast rotation, it does no harm if there is a slight depression between the mast and the leeward side of the sail. The mast can therefore be rotated slightly less; the airflow is nevertheless smooth but head resistance is much reduced. Head resistance is the resistance to airflow exhibited by any

profile. In strong winds the diamonds should be set as slack as possible, but be warned: if they are too slack it may cost you the mast!

It is therefore a question of feeling your way to the 'point of no return' by slackening off the diamonds a few millimetres at a time. That point has been reached when the mast begins to bend in an S in gusts. If your mast shows such a tendency, you should ease the loads on the rig and tighten both diamonds, whether or not this is forbidden. In a Tornado race this may earn you disqualification, but the mast will remain in one piece.

If the jib sheeting position is adjustable, it should be moved outboard and the luff of the jib bowsed down as hard as possible. This keeps the sail flat and allows the airflow to exit cleanly at the leech. The luff of the mainsail is given just enought tension to eliminate diagonal creases; the foot is hauled to the limit by means of the clew outhaul. An open leech is the order of the day.

As the wind increases, the traveller is shifted further to leeward; closehauled, it will be about three hand breadths from the centreline or even further to leeward if circumstances demand – if the wind is very strong it can be set as much as halfway to leeward.

The sheets are not cleated in these conditions; you will need gloves! That goes for the jib sheets too; if wind must be spilled from the mainsail in a squall of force 6 or more, it is essential that the jib sheets be eased as well. If only the mainsail is eased, the excess pressure of the jib rotates the mast suddenly to windward, exerting a load that even the best mast will not withstand.

The reason for such mast breakages, which are typical of many types of catamaran, lies in the static characteristics of the rig. The diamonds and the luff of the mainsail prevent the mast bending too far. If the mainsheet is eased so far

This is how catamaran masts are broken! The tightly sheeted jib backwinds the eased mainsail, creating a reverse camber which in this Prindle has already reached dangerous proportions. If the main sheet is eased still further but the jib sheet left tight, the pressure from the jib's dirty wind can cause the rotating mast to turn suddenly to windward. The support provided by the mainsail luff is then lacking, and breakage is usually the result.

that the mainsail is developing no lift, the luff is no longer supporting the mast. At the same time, however, the correctly sheeted jib is directing an airstream of tremendous force onto the leading edge of the main, rotating the mast to windward (see photograph). The support provided by the diamonds alone cannot withstand such a load, and the result is a trip to the mastmaker.

The same effect occurs in monohulls, though it can be recognised in good time because of the strong backwinding of the mainsail. This is not always obvious in fully battened catamaran sails, particularly if 'the sheets were just eased for a moment in a squall'.

Centreboards and rudder blades are dropped to their lowest position. Before setting out in a cat in strong winds it is essential to check the locking mechanisms once again, for if they are tripped by the tremendous loads imposed on the boards in a strong blow, breakage will be almost inevitable.

Even if the rudder blade does not break, the situation will become critical, for rudder pressure will suddenly become so strong that you will completely lose control of the boat. If you can adjust the tension of the safety releases on your cat, set them as hard as possible in strong winds so that they do not trip involuntarily.

Reaching

When reaching in high winds, the weight of the helmsman and crew must be brought as far aft as possible. The man on the trapeze *and* the helmsman must also secure themselves against sliding forward. The crew should not rely solely on the foot loops, but should also attach the restraining line. Any crew who loses his balance and in desperation holds onto the helmsman deserves the red card, for such behaviour will inevitably drive the lee bow under the lead to a capsize.

The helmsman who believes he can cling onto the tiller for support is also ill

Sitting with legs apart has proved effective for catamaran helmsmen in lumpy seas, particularly on the reach. One foot is placed under the toestrap (the loose end of the mainsheet can be tucked under the boot) and the other is braced forward so that the helmsman does not shoot forward when the lee bow dips in the waves.

advised. Roughened sitting areas on the aft deck have proved useful. The ideal solution is to stick towelling to both the deck and the skipper's trousers.

In this type of sailing it has been found advantageous for the helmsman to sit with his legs wide apart (photograph, page 98), with his aft foot under the toestrap and his forward foot braced against the shroud.

The angle of incidence of the mast can remain as it was on the beat to windward; however, if the crew can stand it, the mast can be rotated as far as it will go and thus set for maximum profile. The diamonds remain in the setting used for beating in heavy weather. The luff of the jib is set slack but free of wrinkles, while that of the mainsail is put under moderate to slight tension; the foot is given a curvature of

> The best way of preventing the leeward hull from burying itself is to keep the windward hull low.

about 20%. As before, the sheets are hand-held so that excess pressure can be spilled quickly from *both* sails in the squalls. The rise and fall of the windward hull are controlled via the sheet; as on the beat, the traveller is set halfway or more from the centreline, depending on the course. With wind abeam, the rule is again to ease both the mainsheet *and* the jib sheet if you do not want to risk breaking the mast.

The danger of the leeward hull burying itself and the possibility of a subsequent 'salto and half turn' is often overestimated. With modern catamaran designs, the danger of this happening is not as great as many experienced cat sailors believe. Cats can be sailed extremely well at the very limit.

An attentive team should be able to do this without great exertion, at least as long as they hold the sheets in their hand. It is essential that the jib be eased first and then the mainsail; easing the jib reduces the pressure and suction on the bows. At the same time, a flapping jib so greatly disturbs the airflow on the leeward side of the mainsail that it becomes less efficient. Only if there is still too much pressure on the lee bow is the mainsail also eased further.

The lifting of the windward hull has another unwelcome side effect besides the undesirable pressure it exerts on the lee hull: the suspended hull and the trampoline, which now has the wind beneath it, provide considerable windage which can contribute greatly to a capsize or a nosedive.

On this course too, the rudder blades remain fully lowered. The position of the centreboards depends on the trim of the boat; a setting between half lowered and fully raised (particularly in the case of the leeward board) will be found to be best. Fully raising the leeward board prevents the lee hull from burying itself if the cat lifts, as it can slide away.

The course is dictated by the wind direction, gusts and waves. Even if the finishing line could normally be laid directly, a zigzag course is sailed.

In gusts, for example, it is advisable to sail a little further off the wind, thereby gaining more speed. If the wind eases, point higher again to maintain speed and return to the shortest track.

Nor can you punch stolidly into the waves head-on without losing momentum. To avoid that, luff up slightly before meeting the wave, bear away on the crest and let the catamaran be carried.

Running

Rule No 1 on this point of sailing: all weight aft! Every ounce too far forward increases the risk. The helmsman will therefore sit more or less on the aft crossbeam and the crew directly forward of him. By both leaning aft or forwards they can lift the tips of the bows when sailing through waves.

The luff of the jib remains as open as possible, so luff tension should be slight. The same applies to the luff of the mainsail. The clew outhaul on the boom is moved well forward to put as much camber in the sail as possible.

If one is tacking downwind, the setting is changed to that described for reaching. The sheets and the traveller are eased right off.

The centreboards are raised fully. Here too, remember that at least the windward board must be lowered by anything up to a half if you launch a tactical attack. One advantage of strong winds is that the range of courses over which conditions are ideal for tacking downwind widens as the wind strength increases. In any case, the sheets are freer than would normally be correct, so that by occasionally tightening them in you can test whether a higher speed could be attained.

If it is blowing so hard that the downwind leg becomes a fight for survival, the prudent helmsman will forget about tacking downwind and will prefer to sail dead before the wind. The laminar airflow generated by tacking downwind places such a load on the rig that the catamaran is more likely to be driven under than if it runs dead before the wind, when the load is also distributed equally between the two bows.

Catamarans with a mainsail that can be reefed have unfortunately become rare. If your sail has a reefing facility, we recommend taking in the reef before the leeward mark so that you can head off on the optimum course immediately after luffing up instead of first having to reef.

Feel again: waves

Waves also call for feel above all else. There is a very appropriate saying in this respect: 'Be kind to the waves and the waves will be kind to you'. It would be difficult to summarise the art of sailing in waves more succinctly or completely.

The general rules to follow are:

- The higher the waves, the less advisable it is to point high.
- Catamarans turn better on a wave than in a trough.

- Each wave has its own rhythm which must be discovered and to which you must adapt.
- The longer the wave, the smaller rudder movements should be.
- Punching through waves always costs speed.

The ideal course through waves will therefore always be a wavy line, which will be more or less pronounced depending on the height and length of the waves (diagram, page 100).

As a rule, the stronger component of the wind/wave combination determines the course: if the waves are the dominant factor, the line will be more sinuous, while if the wind predominates it will be straighter.

It is particularly important to take advantage of the waves on the downwind leg; get it wrong, and you will quickly lose hundreds of metres in relation to those who know how to exploit the waves.

The prime rule is that the cat must have reached the speed of the wave before settling on it. This is achieved by luffing, in other words by sailing an acceleration curve. If the catamaran then sails down the face of the wave it will accelerate, so that the apparent wind will come from further forward, allowing the helmsman to bear away further in a freeing curve. Weight is shifted forward so that the downward slope can be exploited as early as possible. Once the cat is moving down the face of the wave, weight must be moved aft again, as otherwise there is a danger that the tips of the bows will plough into the back of the wave in front as soon as the catamaran is sailing faster than the speed of the waves.

The acceleration that the cat achieves

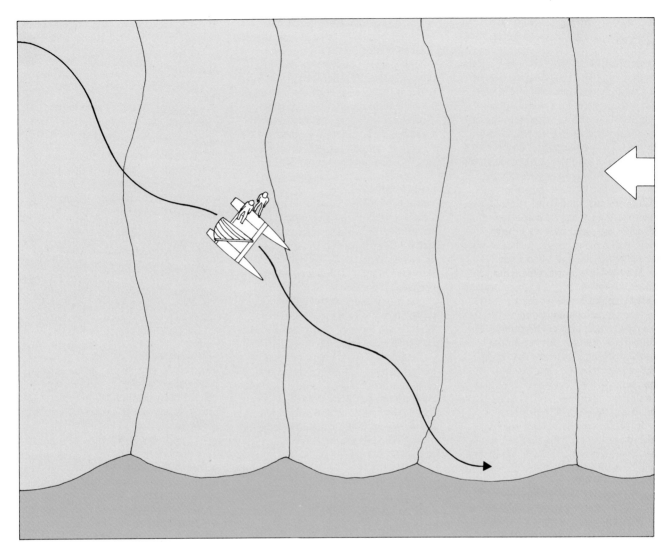

Tacking in waves:

– Bear away before the wave, luff up on and behind the wave
– If you steer in a relaxed and gentle manner, it will also be fun!
– If in doubt, always opt for speed rather than closeness to the wind
– No two waves are the same – each one must be ridden individually

by sailing down the wave must be converted into angle off the wind by smooth rudder movements, with observation of the telltales again playing an important part. If the wave is long enough, you will sail a snaking course down its face dictated by its speed if you wish to stay with it for a long period.

In ideal conditions, you can pick up sufficient speed sailing down the face of one wave to climb over the back of the one in front. This can be achieved by sailing a freeing curve over the entire wave trough. If you miscalculate, however, the sport with the waves begins all over again.

100

Manoeuvring in strong winds

Alertness and concentration contribute much to the success of manoeuvres in strong winds, and they must be applied not only to the speed of the boat but above all to the wind and waves.

The harder it blows, the higher you should point when you begin to tack so that the tacking angle is reduced. Hence before actually going about you should establish how much closer you can sail to the wind without the cat becoming too slow. Watch out for squalls; if you see one approaching, use it to the full but begin luffing before it has past you. In this way, your tacking manoeuvre co-incides with the end of the gust.

It is also possible to tack immediately ahead of a squall, but you must be absolutely certain that the manoeuvre will be completed and the cat moving on the new tack before the squall strikes; for that reason, the manoeuvre is not quite as easy, for the wind veers in the gust and the cat can miss stays. The gust then catches the boat at the worst possible moment, for it is now only partly manoeuvrable.

The ideal gybe curve:

1 After putting the sail across
2 Acceleration curve by luffing
3 Freeing curve by bearing away at the higher speed.

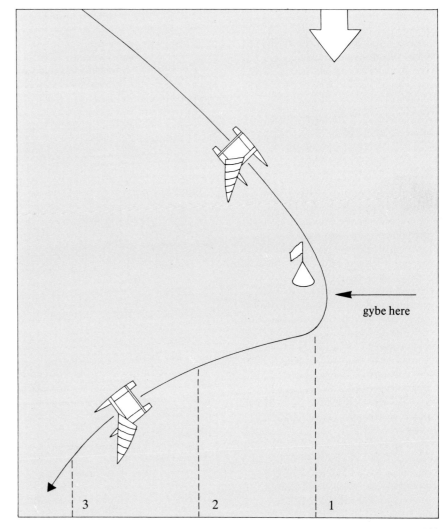

gybe here

3   2   1

The waves are the second consideration when tacking. Try to recognise the wave pattern in good time; where appropriate, keep a lookout for areas of calmer water. These are to be found in the shelter of headlands, in the wake of large ships and, in races, even in the lee of other competitors who are providing momentary shelter. Time the tack so that the turn, when the cat is going through the wind and is making practically no way, occurs exactly on the crest of the wave. However, is is essential to ensure that the boat does not tip forwards uncontrollably, lifting the rudder blades out of the water. The cat should therefore be trimmed by the stern as much as possible, though with sensitivity!

> A stern-heavy catamaran that shoots over the top of a wave can be capsized stern first by the wind under the trampoline.

Speed is the first imperative when gybing in strong winds. The higher the speed, the lower the apparent wind – a general axiom for downwind courses. Repeat this until you are sick of it, for then you will never again get the shakes at the prospect of gybing in a blow.

The course itself demands that the helmsman and crew sit as far aft as possible. However, this is not the end of the story, for if you gybe when the bows are just beginning to slice into the back of the wave in front, you will be in trouble. The rapid change in load from the old lee bow to the new one will press the latter so strongly into the wave that the cat will nosedive and may possibly be pitch-poled.

A swift gybe is the best. The mainsail should go across at precisely the moment when the cat begins to surf down the wave. If the wind is gusty, always gybe when the gust is just beginning to ease.

> Sort out sheets and traveller lines before gybing so that they cannot become fouled!

It is also a common error to sail some distance straight ahead at the apex of the gybe. This produces no benefit, for it is the slowest course you can sail with a catamaran. The apparent wind increases and you have more pressure on the sails than you want. The ideal gybe curve is parabolic (diagram, page 101).

Since you want to sail fast, you need not bother with the reverse rudder stroke necessary on monohulls after the sail has gybed. If you want to round up in any case to sail another acceleration curve, reversing the rudder is superfluous.

> The harder the wind blows, the more important control of the boat becomes. You must be able to execute manoeuvres and trimming adjustments in your sleep; only correct procedures and a lot of practice can help you progress.

The 'survival gybe'

There is one situation that every catamaran sailor fears, and if he is honest he will even admit it: when it is blowing so hard that any deviation from a course dead downwind must lead to a capsize, no matter whether the helmsman luffs or summons up the courage to gybe. In this situation, the 'survival gybe' has proved useful (diagram, right) – though not infallible!

For this manoeuvre, turn directly downwind but try to carry as much speed as possible. Check that sheets and traveller lines run free and bear further away with the mainsail eased right off and the jib flapping. As a rule you will already have the cat on a course up to 135° to the (new) wind direction before the sail slams across.

In this instant luff up smartly onto the new course so that the wind is spilled out of the sail.

Now you can luff up further at your own pace to consider your next move with minimum pressure in the sails, or you can thunder on to leeward.

Study the diagram carefully so that you understand the manoeuvre and can execute it in your sleep. Admittedly, it is rather hard on the gear, but if it is executed properly it almost always prevents a capsize.

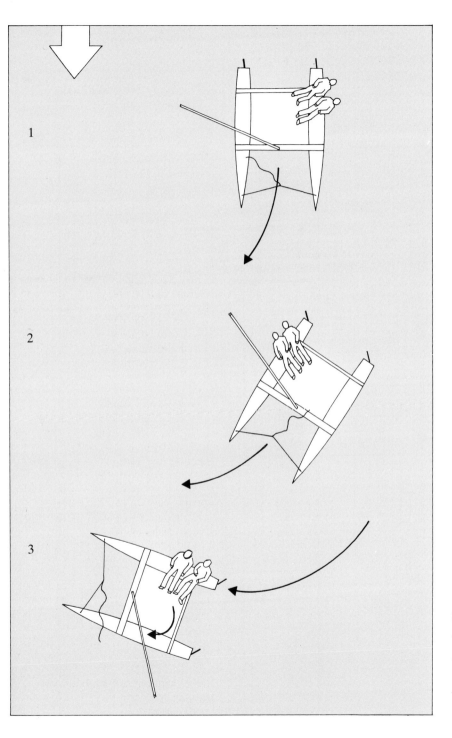

The survival gybe:

1 *On a course dead before the wind clear the mainsheet, the traveller and the jib sheets*
2 *Bear away slowly; before the boom comes across, the crew shift their weight aft onto the future windward side*
3 *When the boom flies across, luff up sufficiently strongly to prevent the sail drawing.*

Trim table

Wind strength on Beaufort Scale	Sitting/trapezing position						Batten tension	Luff			Traveller car		Mainsail foot		
	Helmsman			Crew				Jib		Mainsail					
	To windward	Reaching & broad reaching	Tacking downwind	To windward	Reaching & broad reaching	Tacking downwind		To windward	Reaching & tacking downwind		To windward	Reaching & tacking downwind	To windward	Reaching & broad reaching	Tacking downwind
Light winds up to force 2		on windward hull aft of main crossbeam			on leeward hull forward of main crossbeam		High		Just taut enough to eliminate wrinkles	Always full tension	amidships	Progressively further to leeward until fully outboard when tacking downwind	approx. 5%–10% sail camber	approx. 10%–20% sail camber	maximum sail camber
Medium winds force 2–5		On centreboard case		On leeward hull aft of main beam			Medium	Medium tension			2–3 hand breadths to leeward				
Strong winds force 5–6	Between centreboard case & aft beam	Right aft in front of aft beam		Aft of shroud plate	Trapeze as far aft as possible (restraining line)	To windward on centreboard case	Light	Taut	Just enough to eliminate wrinkles	Just enough to eliminate wrinkles	4–5 hand breadths to leeward		Sail set flat		
Heavy weather force 6–7					Sitting forward of helmsman with foot braced against shroud										
Centreboard position	fully down	between half & fully down	fully retracted												

Coming alongside and casting off

In view of the tremendous acceleration of which catamarans are capable, thinking ahead is the most important aspect of coming alongside and casting off.

There is nothing more amusing for spectators nor more nightmarish for the owners of moored boats and the catamaran skipper himself than the sight of a catamaran flying wildly around the harbour or between moorings while the helmsman desperately searches for an opening.

The first principle must therefore be to execute all such manoeuvres with the minimum sail area necessary to make the boat manoeuvrable.

In practice, this might mean that a Wing will sail to the pontoon with no sail set if it must dock before the wind, since the profile mast itself provides about one square metre (ten square feet) of windage.

The second rule is that a good skipper will always try to keep an escape route open in case the planned manoeuvre misfires.

One point to be borne in mind is that a catamaran has a larger turning circle than a monohull, which can be turned more or less on a sixpence; this is one of the few disadvantages of catamarans.

Remember too that a catamaran gathers way instantly in a gust.

On the other hand, the low weight of a catamaran is a great advantage, as the boat carries little or no momentum and will stop dead after a sharp turn.

Coming alongside (1) a boat, (2) a quay, (3) beaching (a: as soon as the cat has come to a standstill, jump into the water, pull up the rudder blades and haul the boat stern first onto the beach). The manoeuvre should always be executed in such a way that you can run past your intended mooring position and repeat the exercise if the wind suddenly gusts or heads you. No room for false pride here; it is better to try three times!

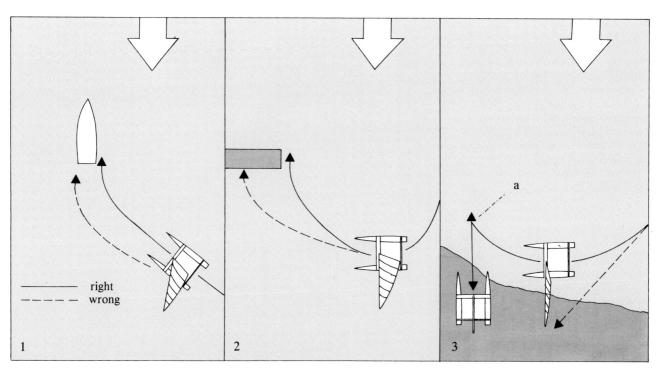

——————	right
- - - - -	wrong

1 2 3

Emergency braking

One well tried method of stopping a cat is to put the tiller over hard first one way and then the other in rapid succession. The braking effect of putting the rudders almost at right angles to the direction of travel is so great that no more than three or four such movements will be needed to bring even a fast-moving catamaran to a standstill, provided the sails are no longer drawing (see photographs). But beware: the cat will then be unmanoeuvrable for a short while!

This method works on courses between closehauled and about a beam reach; of course, at the same time the sheets must be eased right off.

On the beach

Getting under way from a pontoon or from deep water generally presents no difficulties, as the rudders are fully effective from the outset and the boards can also be lowered. Here it is only a question of planning and forethought.

It is different, however, if you must launch from a beach. It can sometimes be a very dicey affair, depending on the strength and direction of the wind and the height and direction of the waves. However, here too the principle is: think first, then act!

Putting the tiller over rapidly as far as it will go will take the remaining way off the boat after rounding up. The left-hand photograph shows the first stage; the boat is still in motion and the rudders are causing strong drag. In the right-hand photograph the catamaran has already almost come to a standstill.

With an onshore wind and correspondingly heavy seas, the passage through the surf is a balancing act. Two points are important: first, the boat must have as much way as possible by the time it reaches the surf line, and secondly it must be steerable, so that the rudders and boards must be at least partly down before you reach that point.

During this phase of the launch the cat must be trimmed as much by the stern as possible to offset the weather helm induced by the half-lowered rudder blades. At the moment when the breakers take hold of the catamaran, the helmsman and crew must shift their weight well forward to avoid capsizing stern-first and the helmsman should luff up sharply to sail through the breakers as squarely as possible. Once the boat is through the breakers, bear away immediately to regain speed. As soon as you have passed the surf line or have reached sufficiently deep water, lower the rudder blades and centreboards fully.

Choosing the correct course from the beach is a great help. The wind almost never blows four square onto the beach, so always launch away from the wind so that you can sail at a steeper angle to the beach or develop more power slightly off the wind. Regattas in coastal waters often have mass starts from the beach. If you are still inexperienced or unsure, first watch those who know the area, but don't be distracted by flying spray and precariously balanced catamarans; pay attention to the angle of launch, rudder movements, the point at which centreboards are lowered and the appearance of the course through the waves. You will then quickly get the hang of it. Bear in mind too that as a newcomer to coastal sailing you should ensure that you have a lot of room to leeward, in other words towards the coast, to avoid colliding with other cats that may launch faster and at a less acute angle than you.

Beaching can really only be a problem if the wind is onshore.

If the wind is not blowing at right angles to the beach, choose the windward side of the wind angle for your approach; in this way you will always run practically dead before the wind onto the beach. You can then raise the centreboards in good time. The rudder blades must be released even before you reach the line of breakers, but it is essential that they remain lowered until the last moment!

It is important that the catamaran always remains at right angles before the breakers and does not broach, otherwise breakage will often occur.

If the beach is stony or steep-to, you have no option but to make a well-timed leap into the water. Luff up sharply, jump overboard as the boat turns and hold it by the bow or forestay bridle until a helper brings the launching trolley. When the water temperature is low you should remind yourself that it is cheaper for the helmsman or crew to catch cold than to repair a holed hull – so it is better to go overboard too soon rather than too late!

If you want to land on a sandy beach you have no problems. Sail dead before the wind until you have cleared the surf and are in calmer water; only then should you turn head to wind and pull the boat onto the beach stern-first. If conditions are light, you can even sail right up to the beach, jump off and drag the transoms above the waterline without getting your feet wet, a manoeuvre for which Hobies in particular have become renowned.

Who likes standing on their head?

Catamarans can capsize – so what? Dinghies also capsize and no-one gets excited about that. The word should have gone round by now that modern catamaran designs can almost always be righted after a capsize – by the crew themselves without outside help.

Modern cats generally have watertight masts that help prevent the boat from turning turtle immediately or even make it virtually impossible, depending on the mast profile and size (see photographs).

Modern catamarans increasingly have such large and watertight masts that the fear of turning turtle has been banished, though the ability actually to stand on the mast, as with a Topcat, is the exception rather than the rule.

The only problem occurs if a catamaran turns turtle. Before buying a catamaran, enquire from the manufacturer or the class association whether the type of boat you have chosen turns turtle easily and whether it can then be righted by the crew alone.

Capsize drill is an important preparation if you want to have fun with the catamaran, particularly in heavy winds.

There is no point practising capsizes in a flat calm, for you are unlikely to capsize for real in a calm. Choose a day with moderate winds, ask a friend with a boat to stand by as a precaution, and ensure that the 'bath water' is of the right temperature. You should also know the depth of water at the scene of the action. As a precaution, choose a spot where the water is at least as deep as the height of the mast, plus a small margin of safety.

An inverted catamaran with a mast that is not watertight is invariably difficult to right. The wind and waves provide valuable assistance that should be used to the full.

Wave action will slowly turn an inverted cat beam on to the waves. Until that has happened, the crew can do nothing but wait, attach the righting line (if one is not carried, the mainsheet will do) and cast off the sheets.

When the cat is lying beam on to wind and waves, the crew attempts to raise the windward hull from the surface of the water by means of the righting line or lines. The wind and waves assist their efforts and the mast and sails prevent sideways drift.

Once the windward hull has lifted and the wind has got under the trampoline, the righting process will gather pace. However, the crew must continue haul-

ing, as wind pressure alone is not enough to bring the mast to the surface. Once you have done that, the rest is easier.

If the wind is not strong enough to help you reach this point, all you can do is to hope for outside assistance.

The brutal method of righting an inverted catamaran by applying sideways force from a motorboat (see photographs overleaf) is not to be recommended with all types of boat, as the load on the points where the towline is attached or bears is enormous, particularly if the motorboat skipper has no

A catamaran that remains on its side like this can easily be righted using the righting line. The righting line (in some circumstances the mainsheet may serve the purpose) should be long enough to give sufficient leverage. In the case of this Topcat it should be no shorter.

experience of this kind of operation, as is usually the case.

It is better to tack a line to a trapeze wire or the halliard and pass it to a helper in a second boat, which could even be a rowing boat. The helper makes the line fast to his boat and motors or rows as far as possible to windward of the cat before hauling in quickly.

The crew of the capsized catamaran assists by sitting out on the leeward hull or hauling on a righting line (diagram, page 112). In most cases this is enough to raise the mast to an angle of about 45°.

A rather rough and often costly method of righting a catamaran that has turned turtle. A towline is thrown from the motorboat to the catamaran and made fast to the shroud plate. The motorboat then pulls with considerable force, often too much force. The high loads involved often rip off fittings or the towline cuts through the hull. The aid that was so welcome at the outset then frequently leads to an unpleasant scene, despite the fact that all involved were only acting for the best.

The helper can now pull it directly upwards, which would not have been possible before. When the mast leaves the water, the helper must grab it and hold on until he has freed the hauling line; alternatively, he could just drop it in the water. The rest of the righting process now presents no problems, with crew and helper working together.

Bear in mind that you must retire if you accept outside help in a race! If possible, notify one of the safety boats of your retirement.

If the catamaran remains on its side, it is first important not to lose touch with the boat, for it will drift to leeward very quickly. Even a strong swimmer cannot catch up in moderate winds,

Up... up... and finally she is floating the right way up again!

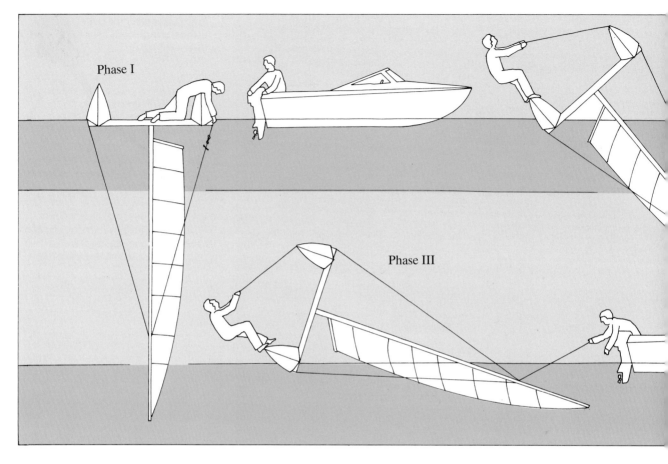

Phase I

Phase III

Righting a completely capsized catamaran with outside assistance:

Phase I

1. Cast off the mainsheet fully

2. *Release the trapeze wire from the shockcord, attach a rope and make it fast to the helper's boat (if the catamaran has no trapeze, lower the sail under water and use the halliard)*

Phase II 3. *The helper rows, motors, or sails **slowly** to windward; the crew assists by using the righting line*

particularly as he is generally hampered by his sailing clothes.

Even if the catamaran remains on its side, you must first wait until the hulls have turned beam on to the wind. This turning motion can be enhanced by shifting weight forward or aft on the lower hull. This is not essential, however, as the cat will adopt this position of its own accord, because the trampoline will act as a sail while the sail dragging in the water will act as a sea anchor, albeit not a very effective one.

There are things that can be done while you are waiting. The sheets must be cast off and the traveller must also be free running.

The righting line (or the mainsheet, if you have no line) is attached to the foot of the mast and led over the upper hull aft of the shroud. The line should be

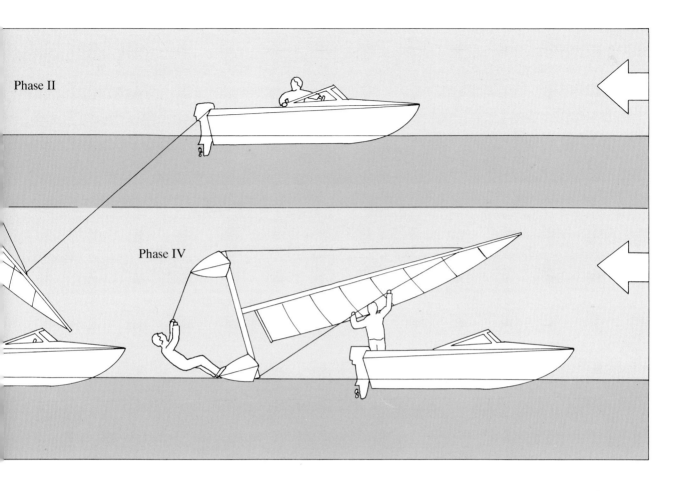

Phase II

Phase IV

Phase III   4. *With the aid of the crew, the helper hauls in the trapeze or halliard hand over hand until he can grasp the mast*

5. *The helper casts off the line*

Phase IV   6. *Assisted by the crew, the helper pushes first the mast and then the shroud upwards until the cat is again floating upright*

long enough for the crew to hang almost horizontally on it at arm's length.

Knots tied in the righting line have proved very useful and kind to the hands. Loops are better still, but they tend to become twisted.

With knots or loops in the line, the rest of the righting procedure is child's play. The crew tries to bring the upper hull down by hauling on the line; they should lean out as flat as possible to develop good leverage.

With practice, righting the cat will

become faster and will call for less effort.

When the hull strikes the water, the safest place for the crew is between the hulls; from there, the quickest way back onto the trampoline is to heave yourself up onto your stomach.

A Hobie 16 demonstrates the art of capsizing: first the lee hull buries itself too far. . .

. . . and the cat keels over. . .

. . . and fall into the sail. . .

. . . but too far aft, so that the sterns go under. This pair are lucky, for in this situation a catamaran will usually turn turtle

. . . sideways and forwards

Now the crew leave their lofty perch with unseemly haste. . .

After much tugging and levering, the Hobie 16 has been brought back onto its side. . .

*. . . albeit so that the wind presses on the **underside** of the trampoline. It would have been better to have waited until the hulls had drifted around the masthead (the sail acts as a drogue); then the pressure of the wind on the **upper** surface of the trampoline would have helped right the boat.*

►

However, this crew is so strong...

...that with the righting lines they can haul their Hobie 16 upright even against the wind

In fairly strong winds, the crew may well find themselves being swept along as they hang somewhere under the trampoline because they are unable to pull themselves back aboard against the flow of water

So do not right the boat until the bows are pointing to windward. Here the manoeuvre has been successful, for one of the crew is already back aboard.

Now it is important to look upwards to ensure you are between the hulls and are not struck on the head.

The series of photographs on pages 114–117 shows the entire sequence of events.

Once back aboard, the first thing to do is to get the boat to lie quietly. As the sheets and the traveller have been freed and the crew weight is forward as a result of the crew climbing aboard via the main crossbeam, the catamaran will usually lie on a course between close-hauled and a beam reach; by working the sheets, it can be kept still until the trampoline has been tidied.

In a capsize, always try not to lose contact with the boat! Think first, then act.

Safety first

In principle, the same safety precautions should be taken for catamarans and their crews as for dinghies.

Lifejackets, not buoyancy aids, should be standard equipment. Good, waterproof clothing that protects the wearer from cold is even more important than on dinghies, for catamaran sailing is a much wetter sport and the stronger apparent wind caused by the higher speeds has a much faster cooling effect.

A towline is not a luxury, particularly as it can be used for any number of other purposes, as a righting line, as an emergency halliard, as a replacement for a broken sheet – and not least as a towline so that the cat can tow you through the water when it is bathing weather.

The main dangers for catamaran sailors are the same as for dinghy sailors: overestimation of one's ability, miscalculation of the weather, foolhardiness.

It is the wind, not the waves, that always presents a danger for small catamarans. So that you can cope if you are caught out by winds of a strength you have never met before, test:

● whether and how well the catamaran will sail under mainsail alone;
● whether and how the reefing system works;
● whether and how well the catamaran will sail under jib alone;
● whether in an emergency it can be sailed under bare poles to a point downwind.

Whatever the wind strength, you should make it a habit to lash down all loose items such as paddles, stowage bags, lifejackets and clothing before setting out and to check over the entire boat while still on dry land.

If your companions get scared, head for the nearest harbour; a petrified crew member is no help at all and may prove a liability. Never sail out to sea alone without telling someone on land and asking them to keep an eye open; and return by the appointed time!

One-man catamarans have one inherent danger: if the skipper falls overboard in light to moderate winds and the catamaran does not immediately capsize, he has no chance of regaining the boat by his own efforts. For that reason, it is imperative that single-handed catamaran sailors wear lifejackets whatever the strength of the wind. This is particularly important if the water is cold, if few other boats are in the vicinity and of course if you sail open waters, such as on the coast.

There are several ways of preventing the catamaran from sailing away from you:

- The helmsman ties the end of the mainsheet round his chest just under his arms (*not* round his waist!). If he falls overboard, the sheet will be hauled in automatically. Ideally, the windward hull will lift and the cat will immediately capsize; if not, it will at least be slowed down so that the helmsman can pull himself back aboard using the sheet.

- The helmsman ties a line round himself in the same way and leads it round the aft crossbeam to the tiller, so that a pull on the line will put the helm hard over, thereby slowing the cat and either capsizing it or making it sail in circles.

- A piece of shockcord is attached to the tiller and tensioned so that the helm is pulled hard over as soon as the tiller is released. The advantage of this method is that the man overboard cannot become entangled in the lifeline, but the disadvantage is that he loses contact with the boat.

The style of world champions: Randy Smyth and James Glaser. Glaser's critical watch on the lee bow has evidently revealed additional reserves of buoyancy, for Smyth is just pulling himself further forward in the shrouds.

Keen competition, coveted honours: Racing techniques and tactics

Racing is the spice in the soup of sailing, even if there is many a fly in that soup, especially for beginners. Catamaran racing has also become highly competitive, and some multihull techniques are completely different from those used in monohulls, so that they need to be learnt and practised.

For beginners, the best training for catamaran racing is still participation in catamaran races. Only by pitting oneself against other boats in the same class over a prescribed course can one demonstrate one's increasing competence and experience through the evidence of better placings.

The very fact that you are a beginner means that you should take part in as many regattas as possible. It does not matter if you bring up the rear; by constantly observing the other boats – preferably those of the good skippers, of course – you can learn more in one day than you could pick up in a week from books.

Concentrate first on your opponents' sail trim (traveller angle, sheeting), and do not neglect weight distribution. Of course, in this respect, you must select a team of about the same weight as you and your crew. Watching others will admittedly cost you places, but the time spent doing so will quickly decrease as your ability to achieve good boat speed increases.

Later, of course, you will have to get to grips with the tactics applied by the experts, but never forget:

> The better the catamaran's speed potential is used, the less you need to bother about tactics.

Preparation

'The regatta begins before I even leave home' – experienced sailors know this and begin intensive mental preparations well in advance of the forthcoming event.

The first thing to consider is the clothes to wear. Choose what you need to take according to the weather situation and the expected water temperature. As a general rule, it is better to take too much than too little, for unneeded gear can be stowed in the car or in the trailer. On the other hand, if you need your wetsuit but have left it at home, that omission may cost you a great many places.

Next, the trailer box (photograph, page 120) or the car boot. Check whether all you need or may need for the boat is actually there.

A well built trailer for a Hobie, though the box should on no account be smaller than this. The after supports incorporate rollers so that the catamaran can be launched direct from the trailer after removing the light board.

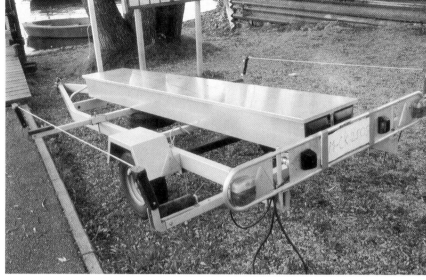

Special sailing directions that it is essential to know are often announced at the pre-race briefing, so it is advisable to attend if possible. However, if your really cannot arrive in time for the meeting, ask your neighbour in the boat park whether any special announcements were made; it may save you a lot of trouble.

You will often find you need a spare split pin when you have just used the last one...

Here is a short list of essential equipment:

- For the crew:
  Dry change of clothing
  Sailing boots or shoes
  Gloves
  Fibrepile suit
  Wetsuit with repair kit
  Oilskin overall with repair kit
  Sou'wester with a chinstrap
  Lifejackets
  Trapeze harness
  Watch
  Knife with shackle key
  Sunglasses
  Suntan lotion
  Lip salve

- For the boat:
  Sails, repair tape
  Battens, spare battens
  Sheets, spare sheets
  Towline
  Spare split pins and rings
  Telltales
  Wind direction indicator
  A few ties
  Gelcoat paste
  Tape in various widths
  Toolbox

In the light of experience, you will yourself add to this list, which is far from exhaustive.

Lastly, before leaving check that you have all the necessary papers: car and trailer papers, driving licence, passport (where necessary), measurement certificate and not least the notice of the race, which you should already have read to see whether any unusual equipment is required. It is also advisable to take the receipt for the entrance fee, if this has been paid in advance.

If you want to arrive at the race venue in good time, you must also set out in good time. Always allow more time for the journey than you would need in the worst contingency. You can never arrive at the club too early, especially if you are a beginner; once you have rigged your boat you have plenty of time to 'spy' on the opposition and learn a lot of valuable tips.

Give yourself plenty of time before the start: it is only after the gun that you need to hurry!

Register with the race committee as soon as you arrive; ask whether the notice of the race contains all the important information, whether there are further details you should know and confirm the time of the pre-race briefing.

When your boat is standing on the launching trolley ready to sail, try to estimate the time you will need to move from the boat park to the starting area. Do not set out too early, for if you must sail up and down behind the starting line for 30 minutes in force 5 winds you will be jaded even before the first beat.

Before dressing to suit the weather conditions, visit the lavatory – you will sail all the better for it!

If you are really short of time, you can finish dressing on the boat as you make your way to the start, but that should be the exception rather than the rule.

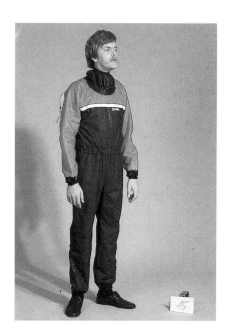

The drysuit has recently gained in popularity because it is light, entirely water and weatherproof, however it is also prone to abrasion and needs protection at main pressure points.

The full trapeze harness is much more comfortable than the trapeze belt that used to be commonly worn, because it supports the thighs and back. When the harness is fitting snugly, the hook should be on or below the level of the navel, never above it.

While on the subject of clothing, note that it should meet essentially three requirements:

It must protect the wearer against heat loss and damp and to a lesser extent against injury. Paper-thin clothing alone is therefore unsuitable. Combinations of fibrepile suits and oilskin overalls or diving suits known generically as wetsuits have proved useful.

Secondly, clothing must be absorbant so that the sailor does not 'stew in his own juice'. Water vapour permeable outfits that let perspiration out but do not let water in are not yet in widespread use.

Finally, clothing must be comfortable. Even if the sailor is wearing several layers, his freedom of movement must not be seriously restricted. The choice of the right clothing has a tremendous effect on well-being. A sailor can achieve his full potential only if he feels comfortable and can therefore concentrate fully.

The same applies to footwear as to other clothing. Surfing shoes are not a bad idea, possibly worn over woollen socks.

Rainproof headgear is not a luxury, as it also contributes to the feeling of well-being. Hoods are not to be recommended, as they prevent the wearer from developing a feeling for the wind. Moreover, they impede vision and hearing, and might therefore be dangerous in a race.

Wet skin is particularly vulnerable to injury, so that gloves are an essential item in a complete outfit. The cheapest and certainly not the worst solution are ordinary household rubber gloves such as one might use for washing up. They are sufficiently tough and generally have a textured palm, so that they provide a safe grip.

Self-inflating lifejackets are not ideal, whether you sail a catamaran or a dinghy. If you do land in the drink, you must sacrifice either comfort (by leaving the jacket fully inflated) or safety (by deflating it). Regatta vests are better, but they should be a snug fit so that they also provide warmth.

It is important for all outer clothing to be conspicuously coloured – yellow, red or orange; white is also the colour of breaking waves!

This regatta vest will not safely support an unconscious wearer, but it is very well suited for catamaran sailing. Quilted permanent bouyancy chambers that fit the body closely give considerable freedom of movement. Surfing boots have proved the best type of footwear.

Closed cell regatta vests have the advantage that if they are damaged no air can escape, as in the case of inflatable lifejackets. The model shown here is also comfortable, which cannot be said of all those on the market, and in addition it keeps the wearer warm.

Pre-launch checks

Before setting out for the start, you should calmly check the boat, its equipment and the crew according to your own checklist. In our opinion, this should include at least the following:

> Are the inspection hatches screwed tight?
> Have all shackles been tightened with the shackle key?
> Have all lines been secured with figure-of-eight knots?
> Are the drainage holes in the transoms closed?
> Is the daggerboard on board?
> Is the paddle on board?
> Is the righting line attached?
> Is the protest flag on board?
> Are the sailing instructions on board?
> Is all clothing on board?
> Watch?
> Compass?
> Is there a snack on board?

This list will grow as you gain experience. Immediately add anything you have ever forgotten and stick the list in the lid of the trailer box.

Tactics

Whereas you will use sailing techniques in an attempt to sail the regatta course as fast as possible, tactics serve to prevent competitors by any *legal* means from doing the same or at least arriving at the finish ahead of you. When Randy Smyth, the world champion in the *Tornado* class, was once asked his opinion of the value of tactics, he replied tersely 'Go fast – and forget about tactics!' Smyth undoubtedly uses tactics too, but he gives them their due place in the order of priorities: first comes boat speed, and only then can one successfully apply tactics. Before getting involved with tactics, you should

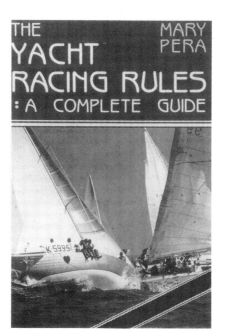

Anyone competing in regattas must have a sound grasp of the rules if he wants to apply tactics meaningfully. Basic information that is also relevant for catamaran sailors is to be found in works such as this.

thoroughly learn and understand the racing rules. It is amazing that even experienced sailors will often engage in tactical duels without being aware of the possible consequences. Such 'anti-tactics' generally have only one result – before you understand what is happening you are disqualified.

The most informative books for beginners are ones that not only reproduce the individual paragraphs of the racing rules but also use phase diagrams to explain at least the most typical situations.

Hence if you do use tactics, you must be absolutely sure that they will have the intended success. If that does not happen, adopt the maxim to 'Sail your own race'!

As a great many good books on tactics in general are already available, we shall confine ourselves to tactics that are typical of catamaran sailing.

Before the start

On the way to the starting area sail a short board to windward to adjust the sails for the prevailing wind strength. Check the setting again by reference to the telltales.

Once everything is shipshape, loiter near the start boat so that you can time the ten minute gun precisely. A una-rigged catamaran lies quietest if the boom is sheeted at about 30° to the centreline and the upper part of the sail is allowed to sag to leeward. But putting the rudder hard to windward, the cat can now be made to luff up briefly and then fall back, so that the boat drifts slowly to leeward with a seesaw motion.

In a two-man catamaran the same effect can be achieved by trimming the mainsail and rudder in the way described for the una-rigged boat and letting the jib flap. In very strong winds

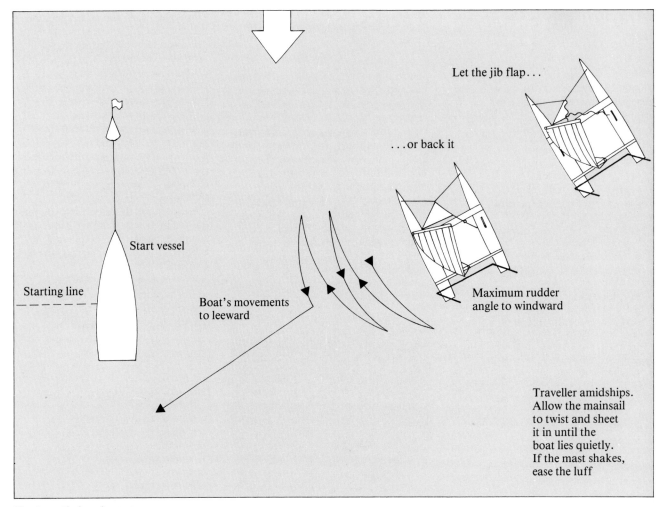

Let the jib flap...

...or back it

Start vessel

Starting line

Boat's movements
to leeward

Maximum rudder
angle to windward

Traveller amidships.
Allow the mainsail
to twist and sheet
it in until the
boat lies quietly.
If the mast shakes,
ease the luff

Heaving-to before the start

the jib can also be backed. In practice, you have now hove to (see diagram above).

Watch out for special signals on the start vessel, such as those for the wearing of personal buoyancy or to indicate a shortened course, the course direction and class. The true course to the windward mark will also often be given on an indicator board; note this down. As soon as the starting line has been laid,

establish whether one side is favoured, keep an eye on the boat laying the buoys and spot the position of the windward mark; this you must know before the start.

Watch the wind for changes in direction and strength. Is it swinging to and fro or shifting steadily in one direction? Are the gusts all coming from the same quarter? Are there particularly gusty areas caused by the topography?

Roughly plan the windward leg accordingly.

Take note of what other competitors are doing and keep clear of one another!

More catamarans are damaged at or before the start than during the race itself.

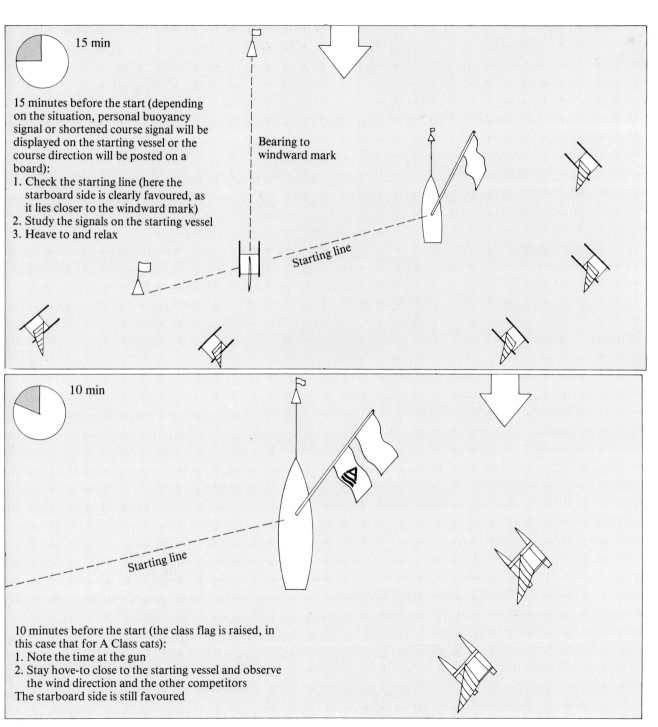

15 min

15 minutes before the start (depending on the situation, personal buoyancy signal or shortened course signal will be displayed on the starting vessel or the course direction will be posted on a board):
1. Check the starting line (here the starboard side is clearly favoured, as it lies closer to the windward mark)
2. Study the signals on the starting vessel
3. Heave to and relax

Bearing to windward mark

Starting line

10 min

Starting line

10 minutes before the start (the class flag is raised, in this case that for A Class cats):
1. Note the time at the gun
2. Stay hove-to close to the starting vessel and observe the wind direction and the other competitors
The starboard side is still favoured

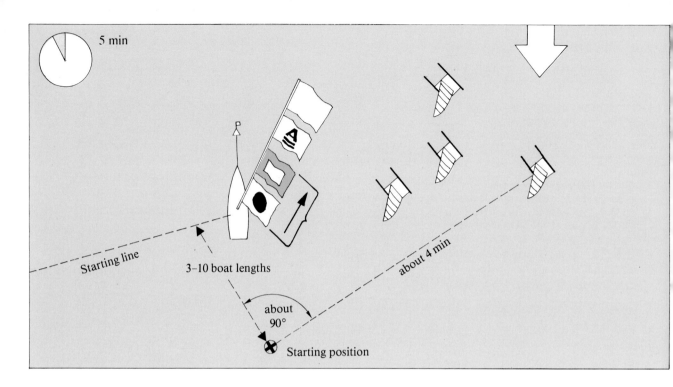

5 min

Starting line

3–10 boat lengths

about 90°

about 4 min

Starting position

Above:

5 minutes before the start (the Blue Peter is broken out – a white rectangle on a blue **ground): and perhaps the 1 minute flag-code flag I (black ball on yellow ground).**

1. Check the time at the gun

2. Position the cat so that in the next four minutes it will drift to the starting position or sail so that it reaches that spot one minute before the start

Depending on wind strength, the starting position is about 3–10 boat lengths from the starting line. From this position you will be able to cross the inner end of the starting line on a normal closehauled course

Right, above:

One minute from the start. (Flag I falls with a sound signal.)

1. Sheet in the sails sensitively and head for the starting line closehauled so that you will reach it in exactly 60 seconds

2. Clip on the trapeze, if appropriate

3. Shout a loud warning to anyone forcing their way in and, if necessary, threaten them with a protest

A, B, C and D, in that order, are in very good starting positions. E, F and G are poised to force their way in and should be warned!

Right, below:

Start. (Class flag and Blue Peter are lowered.)

1. Count the last ten seconds in your head, harden in the sheets and at the gun cross the starting line at speed

2. Do not sail too high immediately after the start; go for speed so that you remain in clear air

A, B, and C have made the best starts. E, F and G have learnt a great deal.

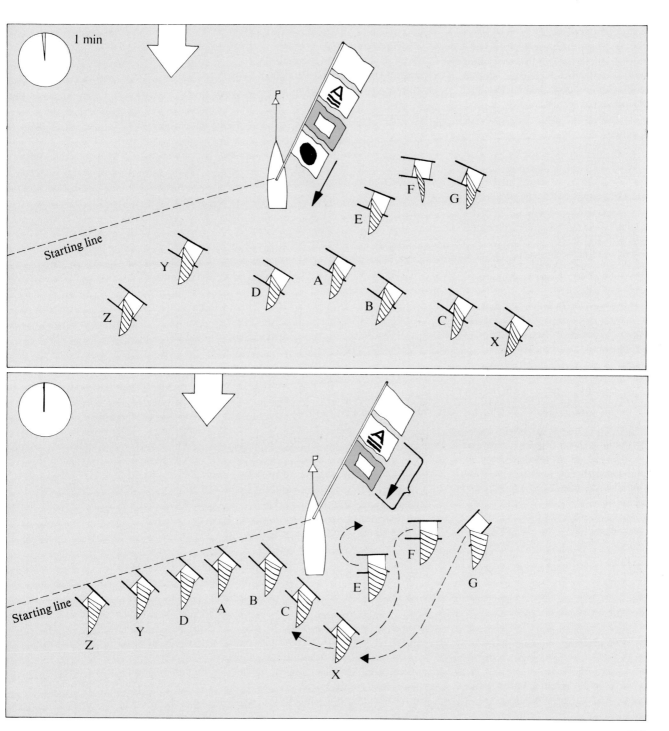

1 min

Starting line

E
F
G
Y
Z
D
A
B
C
X

Starting line

Z
Y
D
A
B
C
E
F
G
X

127

You should have enough time before the starting gun to look over the boat one last time to ensure that everything is really in order. At the five minute gun check that your watch coincides with the signal and then sail slowly to the point from which you want to start. If it becomes clear that the area you have chosen will be too crowded, you should keep clear at all costs; it is better to start in clear wind to leeward of the pack.

Two minutes before the start, set the luff and foot tension and the traveller position as previously determined. By now at the latest you should have decided on your starting strategy; leave it any later, and you will probably not pull it off. Last-minute decisions are seldom the best!

Still remain with minimum way at the spot from which ideally you want to make a flying start. One minute before the start gun the crew clips on the trapeze and you sail slowly towards a position immediately behind the line. Make absolutely sure you still have at least a boat's length of room to leeward to bear away.

About 15 seconds before the start you should be between one and three boat lengths behind the line, depending on wind strength; sheet in the sails so that you cross the line at full speed precisely on the gun.

This is the only method of starting that will enable you to get away really cleanly. Of course, it takes strong nerves to sail towards the line at full tilt; in the early days you will be as nervous as a kitten. Just remember, however, that those who are behind you at the start do not need to be overtaken.

Practise this starting method again and again; almost anything that will give a bearing at right angles to the wind will serve as the starting line: long pontoons, a line of mooring buoys, landmarks, and so forth. With practise, your confidence will gradually increase

and you will be able to shoot for the line with scarcely a qualm.

Do not wait for the gun before hardening in the sheets; the further you are to leeward, the later you will hear the report. As the sails on all those high performance rigs are sheeted home simultaneously, a sudden church-like stillness descends – there's no going back now.

The beat

The first rule after the start is to sail as free as possible. Forget about tactics for the time being; avoid tactical involvements, and especially duels, which at this stage of the race will benefit not just one other laughing competitor but a whole pack of them. Watch the angle to the windward mark closely, but do not go about until you are sure that the long leg has become the short one. Do not tack too often! Each tack costs time and hence distance. At a boat speed of 10 knots you take about 4 seconds to go about; that corresponds to a distance of almost 20 metres (65 feet) or about three-and-a-half boat lengths!

If neither side of the beat appears to be favoured, it is safer to sail down the middle of the course and risk the four tacks you will have to make. From the middle you can watch both sides equally well and establish which has the better wind. Make a mental note of this side for the next beat and for the downwind tacking leg.

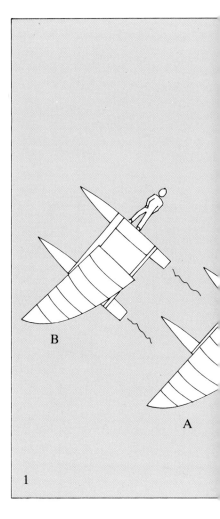

The attack

An opponent ahead of you will always attempt to prevent you passing to windward by luffing to the point of pinching. Follow suit carefully, but on no account sail closer to the wind than your opponent; close up as far as you dare on the basis of past experience. Bide you time in this position until your quarry's attention is momentarily distracted. Then bear away sharply by

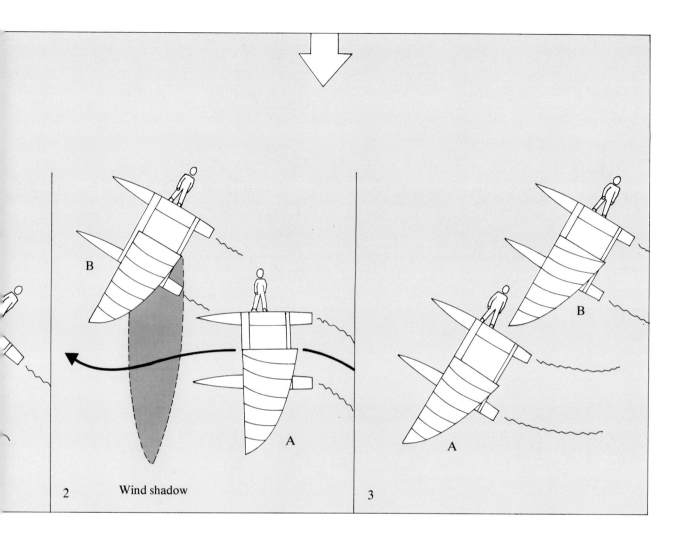

2   Wind shadow

3

about 20°, ease the sails a little and sail well to leeward through his wind shadow (see diagram above and photographs on page 130). This may easily cost you 10 metres (30 feet) to windward, but it is usually offset by the fact that a skipper who once sails too close to the wind will generally continue to do so.

If you want to execute this manoeuvre on starboard tack, estimate in advance whether the remainder of the board is long enough for you to tack before your defeated opponent.

If your target is ahead and slightly to leeward, there is only one way to attack: bear away and try to overtake him to windward thanks to your superior speed.

1. A attacks B: A closes to within about half a boat's length of B.
2. When B is not paying attention or is struggling with a gust, A bears away sharply and thanks to his higher speed breaks through B's wind shadow, extending at least three boat lengths to leeward.
3. A can now continue on his original course at his previous speed. Warning: A no longer has the leeward boat's usual luffing rights over B, so he must build up a sufficient lead to tack safely ahead of his rival.

The breakthrough to leeward, demonstrated by two Topcats. The boat with the white and green sail is attacking the one with the blue sail from astern on the beat.

Blue tries to ward off the attack by luffing.

Here it has worked: white-and-green has managed to break away and can now luff up again, albeit a little further to leeward, and continue on the original course.

The defence

If the attacker is coming up astern and trying to break through to leeward, all you can do is remain alert. Keep a close eye on the helmsman (your crew can attend to techniques and tactics on your own boat in the meanwhile) and follow suit when he bears away to open the attack (photographs, pages 132–133). If he manages to free himself significantly from you and to increase his speed, all you can do is to bear away to match his speed and keep him in your wind shadow.

If your attacker comes from windward and bears away towards you, try to gain speed by bearing away slightly so that you remain in front.

White-and-green initially pretends to luff as well until he is just level with the stern of his opponent; he then bears away sharply behind him.

It is important to bear away enough for the boat to gain speed perceptibly so that it can break through the wind shadow to leeward of your opponent; preferably, time the manoeuvre to coincide with a gust of wind.

If an opponent on the same course is sailing significantly faster than you can manage, let him go.

Concentrate instead on keeping the boat's motion smooth and carefully balanced; every lurch in the waves checks the boat's forward progress.

You should know precisely the angle through which your catamaran will tack; this differs from one design to another, but as a rough guide it will be between about 115° and 125° for cats without a centreboard and around 95° for those with boards. Bear in mind that the angle widens in heavy wind and waves.

Never tack at or around the mark!

A precise knowledge of the tacking angle is particularly important on the last board before laying the mark (diagram, page 132). You should allow between 10 and 70 metres (30 and 230 feet) more for wind shifts and miscalculations, depending on your distance from the mark.

If the windward mark is to be left to port, round it on starboard tack; conversely, if it is to be left to starboard, round in on port tack. Forget about rights of way and inside positions, for the boat that merely bears away around the windward mark without tacking will always have its nose in front.

If the mark is crowded, it is tactically more astute to approach a little further off and to sail around the pack than to pitch into the chaos, even if you have right of way ten times over. Do not steer a tight turn around the buoy, as this only slows the cat down unnecessarily. Bear away gently and try to carry as much speed as possible onto the reach.

Below:
The last tack before the windward mark:
1 *Correct: begin the final tack to the buoy at the right moment! Distance A should be no more than about 1500 metres (1640 yards), as the greater the distance the more difficult it becomes to judge the tack. Depending on distance A, distance B should be between 3 boat lengths and about 70 metres (76 yards).*
2 *Wrong: the final tack was begun too soon! While you are making two additional tacks, your opponents are making good about 50 metres (55 yards).*
3 *Wrong: the last tack has been made too high. Despite the higher speed to be gained by bearing away, B cannot make good the extra distance over A.*

Defence against the breakthrough to leeward: the boat with the light sail luffs behind the one with the dark sail.

Dark pretends to luff as well and keeps a close watch on his attacker.

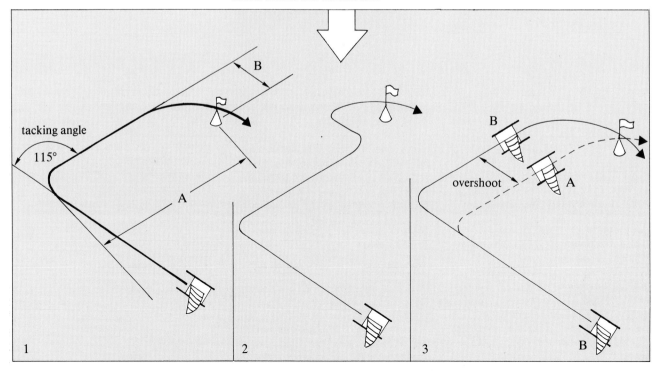

At the instant that the attacker suddenly bears away to begin the breakthrough to leeward, the defender eases sheets and immediately bears away too.

The defender concentrates on keeping the attacker in his wind shadow.

The attacker's attempt to break through to leeward can be regarded as a failure, as he will have great difficulty escaping from this cover.

The reach

If you are free, in other words if you have no opponent in the immediate vicinity, you will sail the direct course to the next buoy at the highest possible speed, concentrating on the telltales and working the sheets continuously.

If you are hemmed in by the pack, try to give yourself room to windward so that you can defend yourself against attack. To do so, it may be necessary to sail a shallow windward curve to the leeward mark.

If you are not under attack, exploit the puffs to gain distance off the wind, for that is essential in warding off any attack.

A leeward curve is advisable only for a boat with a clear lead that can retain its full defensive potential despite the curve. If you have an opponent sitting on your stern, it is better to forget about the leeward curve, or he will have you covered faster than you would have thought possible. If you can afford to sail a leeward curve, then the freer the wind the more beneficial it will be. If the wind is blowing from well over the quarter, you should consider whether a short leeward curve might not free you from a covered position. However, before breaking out to leeward, try to assess whether the boats to windward of you are not about to head away to windward in a luffing duel or a general

windward curve. If so, maintain your course.

> Those who luff must also bear away again, and will then generally lose speed.

As a rule, it is an advantage to sail towards a gust (upper diagram on page 134). However, if the pack is thundering down behind you, luffing in anticipation of the gust brings no benefit, as you will then be in a poor defensive position when the gust does arrive.

It is a real strain on the nerves, but if you have once steeled yourself not to luff until the arrival of the gust, the success it brings will make it easier to be patient in future.

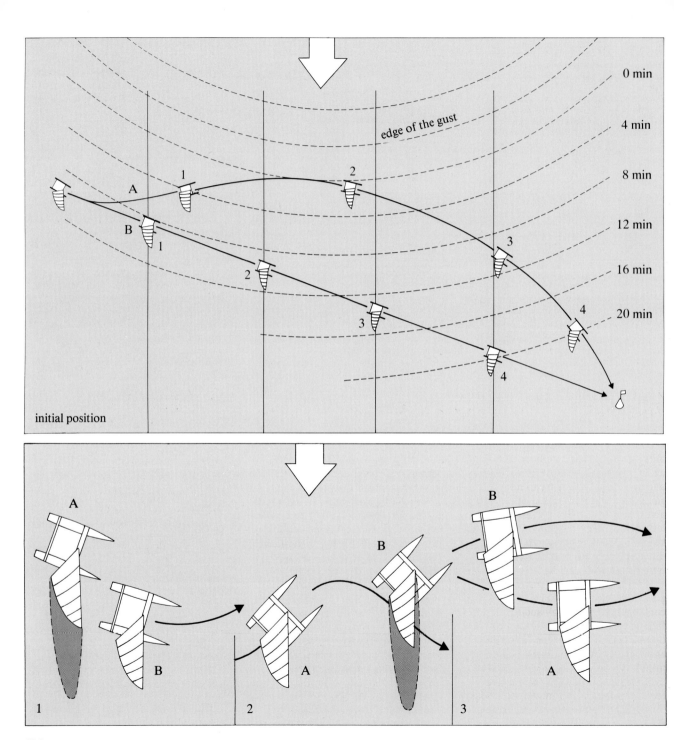

0 min

4 min

edge of the gust

8 min

12 min

16 min

20 min

A

B

initial position

134

Reaching course with gusts
Initial position: A spots the gust and luffs towards it, while B continues on the shortest track. By luffing, A is already sailing faster
1 *A has already reached the gust and will now accelerate noticeably despite bearing away. B continues at the same speed, unaffected by the gust*
2 *A can sail faster and further off the wind in the gust; B has still not felt the gust*
3 *Only now does B reach the edge of the gust*
4 *Now B is sailing slightly faster than A, but can no longer close the gap before the mark*

Left below:
The attack on the reach
1 *A attacks B, trying to bring B into his wind shadow by overtaking to windward. B will normally respond by luffing*
2 *The feint: A pretends to luff as well, gains speed (if possible with the aid of an additional puff of wind) and uses the greater momentum to break through the relatively narrow wind shadow to leeward of B*
3 *By the time B realises what has happened, A must be so far ahead that he in turn may luff A (in accordance with the mast abeam rule of the International Racing Rules)*

The attack

The best opportunity for a successful attack comes in a strong gust, preferably one that is not too short. Once again, approach your victim very closely and as the gust strikes try to luff smoothly but positively, to gain speed and to overtake to windward (diagram left, below). Pass him fairly closely, so that you can slow him down by spilling dirty wind into his sails and keep him under control.

If the defender reacts correctly and in good time by luffing, the gust will enable you to bear away and to sail a freeing curve faster than your opponent, as you have virtually sailed an acceleration curve. Almost the most important part of this manoeuvre is to avoid unnecessary movement aboard, for only a boat that is moving smoothly through the water has any chance of sailing faster than its rival.

The defence

Take up the challenge only if you are sure that a duel will not lose you several places (for instance, in the meantime a whole pack of other boats may break through to leeward).

The important point is to recognise immediately when a following opponent luffs. Watch the helmsman closely, especially the way he manipulates the tiller, as this will give the first signs of a change of course. Your reaction will always be fractionally later than your opponent's initiative, and should therefore be rather more vigorous than the attack.

Try to keep your opponent under control until the gust has passed; after that you hold the better cards.

More important than the defence against a single opponent is the defence against a pack preparing to overtake to windward (diagram, top of page 136). If you do not manage to parry the attack, you will slip back several places. Hence, watch very carefully whether the boats following to windward are beginning to point higher to gain the necessary speed for this manoeuvre. The ideal position from which to mount a defence is slightly to leeward and ahead of the pack; you should manoeuvre into this position in good time so that you can calmly ward off a concerted attack.

Whereas the breakthrough of a single opponent is not so disastrous and can therefore be tolerated from time to time, defence against a mass attack is a must!

At the gybe mark commence the gybe gently so as not to lose too much speed; if your momentum is checked too abruptly you are almost bound to slip into the wind shadow of the following boats. Even if you gybe around the mark very quickly, look to the following boats immediately and sail well clear of their dirty wind.

Observation of the field behind you has another advantage – it is impossible to overlook any gusts that occur and their strength and direction can be determined precisely. If you spot a gust, sail towards it immediately. The closeness to the wind you will lose can generally be more than made up by bearing away in the gust.

Approach the leeward mark in a wide arc (diagram, bottom of page 136) so that you can begin the beat after luffing up close to the mark. As you head up before rounding, trim the rig and the boat for the windward leg, so that after the buoy you can sail an optimum close-hauled course without any loss of time.

For the same reasons you should never gybe round the leeward mark. Even if you follow the ideal track round the buoy (which is more than questionable) you will certainly not have time to adjust the trim for the beat. Hence, you should luff up slowly so that you gain

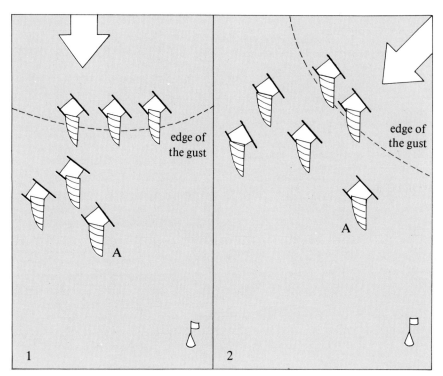

The pack bears down from astern in a gust:

1 *with wind from well astern:*
   A must keep his nerve and continue along his course until the edge of the gust reaches him too.
2 *with a quartering wind:*
   A should move to windward to reach the edge of the gust and then bear away again at higher speed.

1

2

edge of the gust

edge of the gust

A

A

Rounding the leeward mark without opposition. Only those who approach the buoy from well over on the outside of the course can then luff up close to the buoy and save ground to leeward.

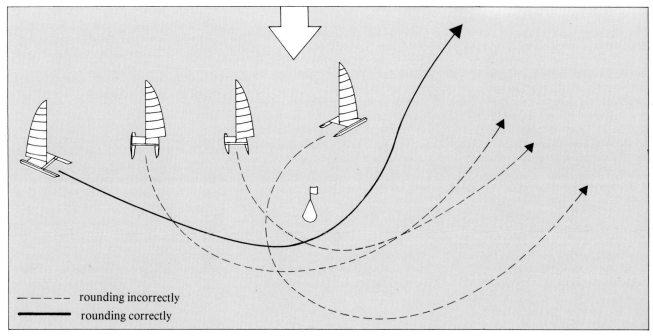

- - - - - rounding incorrectly
———— rounding correctly

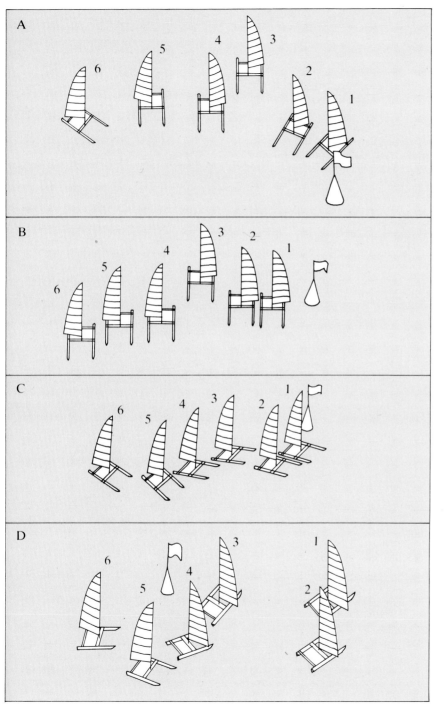

Rounding the leeward mark in a pack:

A. The developing chaos. Although 1 and 2 are in the right-of-way position, they are too close to the buoy to round smoothly

B. Except for number 3, none of the boats can turn, as none has free water on the bows. Only 3 was able to keep its bows clear by means of 'emergency braking'

C. The courses of all except 3 and 6 are dictated by overlaps. Because of their large turning circle, 1 and 2 fall away well to leeward, while 3 can harden up immediately at the mark

D. Keeping clear has paid dividends for 3 and 6; 1 and 2 have had to pay for their mistakes.

speed rather than losing it.

If you arrive at the leeward mark in a pack of boats, your maxim must be 'room to leeward'. Without that room, chaos and breakage are on the cards. You can therefore happily forego the shortest route and sail outside the pack round the buoy (diagram, page 137). Although inside boats have the right of way, it makes more sense to skirt the bunch and then steer towards the inside; the previous inside boat cannot round the buoy so closely that you will not have room to harden up under his stern and begin the beat from a more advantageous position. In such situations it is popular for the boat that was on the inside before the buoy to bear away towards you to block your manoeuvre; make it unmistakeably clear to the skipper that his action contravenes the rules. If necessary, you can give a quick touch on the brakes.

If there is bunching at the leeward mark, always stay outside and approach the buoy wide so that you do not give away any ground to windward for the beat.

On the downwind leg

The criteria for manoeuvres at the leeward mark obviously also apply when the fleet reaches the buoy at the end of the downwind leg.

Tactical duels are extremely rare while tacking downwind. This is easy to understand, for an optimum downwind tack produces more than even a dozen successful duels and the danger that a whole group of other laughing competitors will slip through to leeward while you are setting about an opponent is greater than on any other course.

The most important tactical advice on this course must therefore be to sail your own race. Obviously, this includes watching your opponents.

The first board of the downwind tack is generally determined by the course from which you bear away at the windward buoy, but you are free to choose the final board. If you are wise, you will ensure that it will lead you round the leeward mark without gybing. You should gybe far enough from the buoy to give yourself at least room for an acceleration curve (diagram, right). However, do not leave too wide a margin, as the order of rounding often does not become clear until just before the buoy, especially if you have little race experience; in this way, you may still be able to catch this or that opponent.

On a direct course downwind every duel costs distance, and distance is the factor that must be kept to a minimum on the direct course to leeward in light winds. Undoubtedly this or that crew will be better than you on this course; one has only to think of the extreme lightweights that a heavier crew can never match dead before the wind. Let such boats pass you and try to keep out of their wind shadow as far as possible.

On the downwind leg it is boat speed that counts first; tactics should take second place!

The final beat

'Races are won on the finishing line'. True enough, but the basis for victory is laid throughout the race, not just on the final beat.

As a rule, the field is so spread out when the leading boats begin the final beat that only one or two boats ahead of you can still be caught. However, in view of the greater distance between individual boats, a tactical duel is generally easier on the final beat, as one rarely has to fear losing too many places. Sound tactics on this leg demand that even before rounding the leeward mark you have recognised where the finishing line lies and whether one side is favoured, which is nearly always the case. If you have no opponents within your immediate vicinity, you then sail your own race towards that end of the line.

The attack

If your opponent cannot be beaten on speed, usually all you can do is to sail an extremely long tack. However, it is important that there should not be a third boat dangerously close that may finish ahead of you if the ruse fails.

For a ruse it is. Anyone sailing an extremely long tack hopes that the

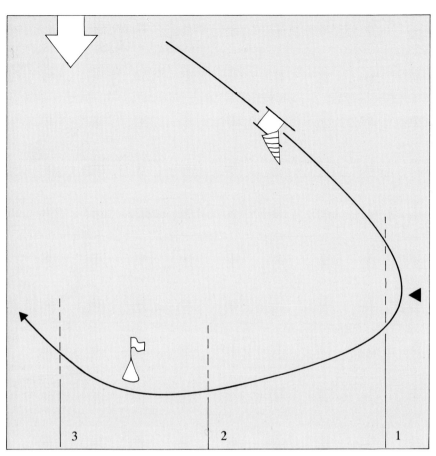

Gybing round the leeward mark

1 Gybe here
2 Acceleration curve
   – adjust the traveller for the upward leg
   – lower the centreboard
   – tension the foot and luff for the beat
   – begin to sheet in
   – rotate the mast
3 Make a smooth rounding
   – after the mark head up into the wind
   and as far as possible trim the sails for the
   upwind leg
   – make fast the sheets

helmsman of the leading boat will become nervous and make a tactical error that will allow one to break out of his control. Of course, there is also the chance that the long tack will bring some advantage, but one should never bank on it! Do not bother with the 'dummy tack' popular with many keel-boat sailors, for the time lost with multihulls is so great that this trick hardly ever succeeds.

The defence

If you have an opponent hard on your heels during the final beat, it is essential to keep yourself between him and the finishing line so that your options remain open.

If the following boat is not very close, you can content yourself with remaining between him and the finishing line; this is termed loose covering. On the other hand, if he has closed up, make sure you are always to windward of him (tight covering).

The tighter the cover, the more accurately must the helmsman of the defending boat sail, and the closer the finishing line the harder must he concentrate on covering. It is then the crew's job not only to keep a close eye on the trim of the boat but also to pay attention to other boats and possible wind shifts.

> If your loose covering is good, you will often not need to do tight covering.

Strong nerves are a trump card for both attacker and defender, more so on the final beat than during the earlier stages of the race. Helmsman often literally throw away several places only metres from the line. Once you have crossed the finishing line, on no account recross it, as you will almost certainly be disqualified. This has been the fate of many in the moment of elation at a good result.

> Not until your own position in the field is absolutely clear can you successfully concentrate on individual opponents.

What's what on the catamaran?

*The Tornado, which has all the modern
trimming gear, is typical of all fast racing
cats. The mainsail is loose-footed and the
rotating mast is held in the correct position
by a mast spanner. Like most catamarans, it
has a lock at the masthead for the main
halliard, generally a hook into which a ring
on the headboard or halliard automatically
engages when the sail is hoisted. The jib luff
tensioner is led via blocks along the hulls to
the main crossbeam. (Diagram reproduced
from The Hardbook of Sailing by Bob
Bond, London 1980)*

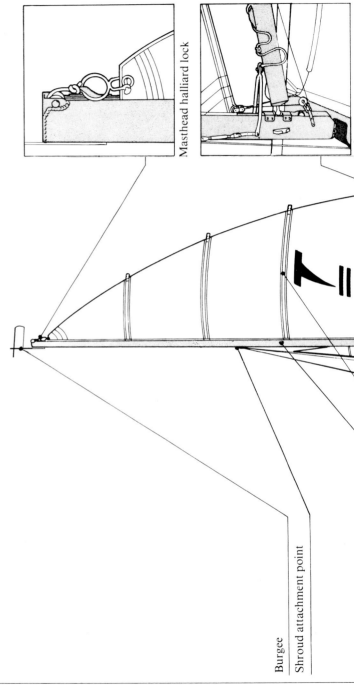

Masthead halliard lock

Mast spanner

Burgee

Shroud attachment point

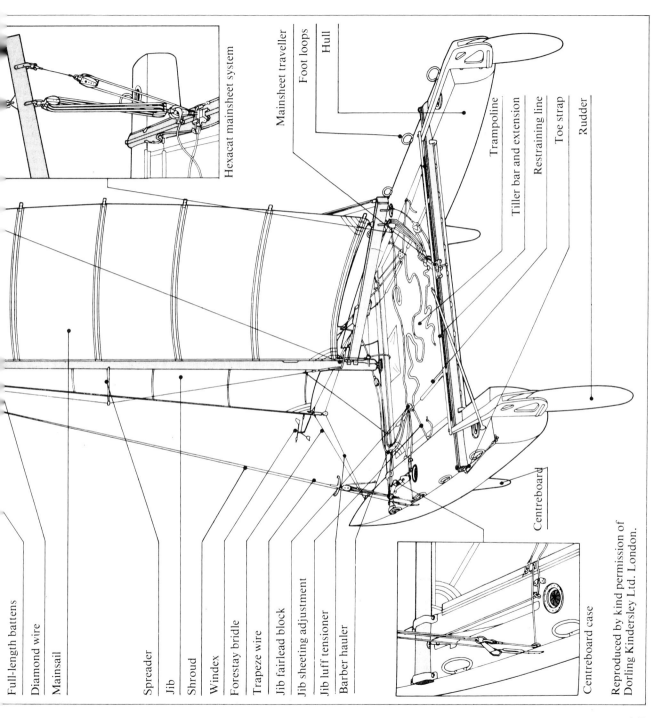

Full-length battens
Diamond wire
Mainsail

Spreader
Jib
Shroud
Windex
Forestay bridle
Trapeze wire
Jib fairlead block
Jib sheeting adjustment
Jib luff tensioner
Barber hauler

Hexacat mainsheet system

Mainsheet traveller
Foot loops
Hull

Trampoline
Tiller bar and extension
Restraining line
Toe strap
Rudder

Centreboard

Centreboard case

Reproduced by kind permission of
Dorling Kindersley Ltd. London.